Wind Drinker

~ Dreams that last forever
are those we never live ~

js

Wind Drinker

By
Jefferson Spivey

Sabertooth ® *Press*

Sabertooth ® *Press*
9244 West Wilshire
Yukon, Oklahoma 73099-8322

Second Edition 2007
Revised and expanded. Contains 102 photographs.
(First Edition 1999)

Cover design, text layout, poems, songs and verses by the Author.

Cover, front & back – Jefferson Spivey & his horse Mr. Sol – 🎥 R. Madden & js

Printed in the United States of America

Wind Drinker

Dedication

To Kristine and Allison and to my children –
Jeremy Adam, Tecla June and Aaron Christian

Also –
For the dreamers and the doers and especially
for those who are one and the same.

Acknowledgments

There are people in my life who are permanent images in my mind. Like an old movie, I see them all the time. Though some are gone, they will always be there and will never change. Here are some of the good ones, not necessarily in the order of their greatness.

Charles A. Codding
G. W. Blevins
George Salamy
George A. Gardner
Harley V. Duncan
Harvey W. Tedford
Jerry D. Brown
John & Donna Rohloff
John J. Spivey
Joseph H. Stuever
Kimball J. Darbe
Luwanda McKinney
Max Evans
Tracy Kelly
Added thanks to Harley

Preface

My first horseback journey began at the Pacific coast on the beach at Santa Barbara in April 1968. I wanted to find the America I grew up reading about. I was fearful that it would be gone. While living mostly off the land, I rode through all the seasons and across four thousand miles. It took seven months to reach the Atlantic. It was not my intention and I did not realize at the time, but what I had done was a first – one man on one horse across the continent in one continuous trek. When I returned home the National Cowboy Hall of Fame honored me.

I started another journey in 1971, this time in a donated four-wheel drive Toyota Land Cruiser. With a grant from Defenders of Wildlife I set out to investigate the best way to establish a system of trails throughout the nation. The project covered six months and twelve thousand miles.

In 1984, I saddled my horse Najah, and took another ride from Canada down the Rocky Mountain chain to Mexico, basically to promote the trail concept that I had started in 1971. It was to be a nationwide network of non-motorized, interconnecting trails with state and national park sites as hubs for the system. And, it was another first, having crossed America on horseback west to east and north to south.

And in 1985, I rode a thousand miles carrying a letter of support from the Governor of Oklahoma to the Governor of New Mexico. It was an attempt to connect the two capitols with the first leg of Freedom Trails by following the Canadian River, abandoned strips of old highway 66, railroads and streambeds.

I was invited to bring my trails concept to Namibia, SouthWest Africa, in 1986. There, I rode on horseback across the empty badlands with an American companion, Bayard Fox and seventeen soldiers of the S.W.F. Special Forces.

In response to a growing interest, I have written about a unique knife I invented during my first ride. The Cowboy Hall of Fame commissioned a limited edition of the Sabertooth knife that has subsequently become a registered trademark. Also, I reference a new saddle design.

My reason for writing this book started with the hundreds of letters stuffed in file cabinets inside my garage. That is where most of the correspondence ended up over the years. Obviously, there was a lot of interest in what I have done. And, for that reason, this book was initially conceived as a how-to-book, to answer all those questions. I decided the only way to get anyone to read a how-to was to include the story of my first ride. When I made that ride, I knew nothing of what I was getting into and I want the reader to experience the uncertainties, as I did, of what lay ahead. Also, I touch upon aspects of my other rides. By the time I rode from Canada to Mexico, I was sixteen years older and definitely wiser. This Second Edition has enabled me to tie up loose ends left dangling in the First Edition. For a greater pictorial account, ninety-three photographs have been added to the previous nine.

As this is a book of memoir and instruction, I have included passages from logbooks and audiocassette tapes that I carried on various treks.

Early in the journey I began to think of my horse more as an equal, than a beast of burden. Consequently, I spoke to him often. So, when to the reader, I seem to be alone and the words *us* or *we* are used, the references are to my horse and me.

Wind Drinker is the story of an innocent blundering that led to an epic journey. It was a life-changing event and this is an account of why and how it happened.

Desire and determination blazes the path of experience.
But, old trails fade for the followers, who then must blaze their own.

js

First Edition, winter 1998
Second Edition, spring 2007

Contents

With the exception of the cover, photographs formatted in black & white and cropped for this book have otherwise not been changed. In place of the word photographer, the image of a camera is used. (📷)

Taken by the Author (📷 *js*) or with the camera he carried.

Part One

Mojave Desert

A Mojave wind blew walls of sand through dry-brush dunes and it was getting stronger. I was in the middle of it all, leading a horse and pack mule, aimlessly pulling them both in the gray desolation. I paused on the edge of a shallow streambed and squinted over the bandanna covering my face. No water! I looked at the animals. Their closed eyelids were trembling and their tails were tucked in tight against the growing wind. I lowered my head in despair.

It was getting late. I untied the makeshift packsaddle, an Army duffle bag, and let it fall to the ground. I left the horse saddled and fearful of losing him and the mule, I tied the lead rope and reins to my wrist. Then, the storm hit, a stinging blackout. I turned my collar up, drew the animals closer and went to my knees.

"We wait it out guys."

There was a faint whistling sound. It grew to a roar then burst like thunder overhead. I took my hands from over my ears as two fighter jets hurtled low through the growing darkness. The animals moved forward, with me between them and settle down.

God, what am I doing? I went over, on my side and buried my face in folded arms. *Gotta find water!*

I closed my eyes, there was a bright flash. It was sunlight dazzling through gushing water. The smiling face of my wife was there, mischievous and giggling. I could see her brown eyes and wavy, auburn hair. We were together on the driveway of our apartment washing the car. Out infant son Aaron was there too, sleeping in the shade. I pointed at my open mouth and Kristine splattered my face with water. The images faded and the wind took its place. I let out a helpless, angry whine.

"Am I... insane?"

Kristine Cynthia Spivey *js*

I woke up and looked around, it was morning. My eyes cringed in the bright sunlight. It was calm and clear and quickly growing hot. A passenger jet rumbled toward L.A. International. All aboard had lots of water I thought, large glasses tinkling with ice. I considered turning the animals loose. Without me maybe they could find water. But it was just a thought. Doing such a thing would have been too final. It would have meant giving up. A year of planning dashed and all doubts confirmed. Then, there would be a sick feeling, it would hid inside and nag me for the rest of my life.

The windstorm had blown itself out. My legs were practically covered with sand. As I lowered my head, something caught my eye. Two mice appeared on a mound in front of me, leaping and tumbling, having a great time. They looked at me and scented the air. Then I noticed something else, the wind was rising again. Sand from the frolicking mice sprayed my face. I dried my eyes with a bandanna and got to my feet. With sand pouring from my clothes I unwound the lead rope and began shedding weight.

I had started at Santa Barbara and already I had gotten rid of my first mule. I had mailed the packsaddle with most of my supplies to Manitou Springs, over the Rockies. Here I was, still in California's Mojave Desert, getting rid of more things. Items I once thought I could never do without. I considered a large bottle of Cornhuskers lotion, and then tossed it aside with the rest of the stuff.

I pulled a map from my pocket, and searched for my position in a blur of contour lines. I closed my eyes and waited for the feeling to pass. A gust of wind snatched the map from my hand. It slapped against the mule and made him jerk back fearfully. Then, it slammed into a bush and hung there for a moment. I watched helplessly as the map went tumbling across the flats out of sight. At that moment, and for the second time, everything went black.

I could not have been out long. I felt a tugging at my wrist. When I looked, my hand was rising and falling, still tied to the reins of my horse. My left hand was empty and the mule was gone. The awareness of what had happened and the fear of losing all that was left got me to my feet. With an extra wrap on the reins I followed the mule's tracks.

We paused at the crest of a swell. The mule had found water. Maybe bad water, I thought. He was drinking deeply. Clinging to the reins of my horse, I drew my gun and fired skyward. It did no good. I aimed and fired again. The bullet hit inches from the mule's nose. He merely backed away, and then moved in again to drink. It was hopeless. "Stupid!" I raged.

Fearing another storm, I kept watch on the horizon as the sun went down. So weary and hopelessly blundering, I would not even roll out my sleeping bag. As the night closed in and the air grew cold, I went about shivering in my defiance.

I was camped against a brush thicket where my horse was tied. Using pliers, I lifted a can of boiled water, let it cool and then poured it carefully into the waterbag. I added a small bottle of English military purifying tablets and sloshed them around. For the first time in three days, the army surplus waterbag was nearly full. As I went to refill the can, I paused to observe the mule. His feet were spread apart and his head was down. His eyes were half-closed, and his nostrils pulsated with each breath. On our first day out, I had noticed the mule's droppings laced with blood. And, unable to respond appropriately, I simply continued, hoping for the best. This was my second mule. My first mule, Sunflower, wouldn't pack. I had sold her for fifty dollars and used the money to buy the one now swaying before me. I was a little worried when I laid eyes on this somewhat scraggly looking animal.

"Don't let his looks fool ya," the man had said, as his Indian wife reached for the money. "He's a good packer."

"Get better! Okay?" I continued on to fill the can.

With the waterbag strapped to my shoulders and my horse loaded with the extra gear, we struck out in the darkness. Sixty yards out, I took off the waterbag and tied the horse. "Wait here," I told him.

The moon was on the western horizon and dawn lit the east. I drew back the hammer of my Colt, aimed and gritted my teeth.

The loud blast reverberated and along with the fluttering sound of an owl it faded. I hadn't had the mule long enough to give him a name. Plagued with guilt I went for my horse.

4

An hour later I halted at the base of a long rising hill. I sized it up, but I was too weak and tired and decided to rest before attempting it. The straps of the waterbag were growing more painful. I had been using my thumbs to keep the straps from rubbing the same places on my shoulders. Broken blisters and fresh blood soaked the shoulders of my blue shirt. I tied the reins to the stub of a bush and let the waterbag settle to the ground

I took the gun from my holster and sank down. I opened the loading gate, turned the cylinder and ejected the spent cartridge. The gun and I had come a long way together, I thought to myself. I had purchased it six years earlier. I used it to teach and debunk gunfighter legends of the old west. Now subsequently, the gun had taken on a more serious role. It slipped from my hand. I rolled forward and curled up beside it. As I lay there burning, I just wanted to sink into the sand, blend into the earth around me.

If the water was going to kill me, I decided, it would be here in this solitary place. My attempt will be, just another Mojave tale.

Desert dawn.   *js*

Jefferson Spivey.

Hollywood California

My gun was spinning horizontally in the blue sky above my head. I reached up and my hand intertwined with the stag-handled Colt. Twirling it fast, I brought the gun down slowly and it slapped smoothly into the holster.

Cinematographer Hedy Dietz, who owned a small production company called Four-Star, secured his camera and came forward. He handed me a twenty-dollar bill and we shook hands.

"That's it, Jeff. It'll look good in slow motion. Thanks for coming out."

"Anytime!"

"Still writing?"

"Yeah, still."

"Did you get an agent?"

"No, not yet."

"Well, keep at it."

We parted company. I put the money in my shirt pocket, took off my gun and started across the studio grounds. Halfway across the lot I noticed something and stopped. A tiny flower grew in a crack of the asphalt at my feet. I bent down and touched the tiny blossom and searched the giant back lot for more such flowers, but there were none. In fascination, I stood and backed away.

In North Hollywood, I dashed across Ventura Boulevard and leaned into the open window of Yellow Cab 3059. I put my holstered gun in the seat and straightened up with my Yellow Cab hat and sunglasses. I put them on and looked up and down the street for a prospective rider. There was no one afoot. So, in the colossal mix of cars, freeways, buildings and heat waves, I deadheaded back to the Hollywood Cab station.

I was a writer in Hollywood; at least that's why I was there. To pay the bills, I worked at whatever I could find to survive. My first place of lodging was an eight-dollar-a-week room at 1800 North Western Avenue. It was a boarding house but I did not have a job so I could only afford the room. Finally, I got a job at the Continental Hotel on the Sunset Strip, and moved to an apartment.

The owner of the hotel was ex-cowboy superstar Gene Autry. He also owned the Los Angeles *Angels* baseball team. His wife, the former Ina Mae Spivey, was my cousin, so getting the job was smooth sailing. I was given a red uniform and posted at the front door where I met them all, the has-beens, wannabes, would-bes and the stars.

Ina Mae, who had insisted I call her just Ina, routinely picked me up on Sunday morning in her gold Cadillac. We would go to church and afterwards, to Beverly Hills for lunch, where no more than a nod from Ina, paid for it all. There we would reminisce about our family history that, except for a little on my side, I knew almost nothing about. Though Ina was of my mother's generation, she was my first cousin. Her father, my Uncle Barney, was the oldest of six brothers. James DeWitt, my father, was the youngest and for that reason he and Barney were close.

Again, it was one of those Sunday mornings, and though Ina and I had been together many times before, this time we spent the whole day exploring the past. She wanted to know all about me.

When my father died, my mother, Audrian Eudora Spivey, whose friends called her Dora, was left with six children. The older three, Lillie, Leon, and James DeWitt Jr. were able to fend for themselves. That left Merle June, John, and me. I was the youngest and the three of us were put in an orphanage. My years from toddler to adolescent were spent in orphanages and schools in Bethany, Ponca City, and Watonga, Oklahoma. At the age of four, I was featured on the cover of a booklet put out by the Catholic Charities, looking ragged and forlorn. I found one of the booklets. My mother had written on the picture – *This is my baby*.

Merle June ran away from St. Joseph's Orphanage long before John and I did. Though born with the natural talent of an artist, Merle June was presented with two options to survive. Go back to the orphanage or get married. She married at the age of fourteen and spent most of her creative years raising a family and merely dabbling at the fringes of the artist dream. The man she married was an alcoholic. He abused her during her childbearing years. That is, until I grew old enough to put the fear of God in him. I realized very young the importance of family for precious shreds were all that was left of mine.

By the time I was eleven, my brother John and I had run away from two orphanages. John went off to Korea as a Combat Engineer with Oklahoma's 45th Infantry Division, and came back a hero to us all. He and his new wife Nadine, also raised in an orphanage, immediately settled down to family life with ingrained determination – their children would never go to an orphanage.

I joined the Marine Corps just before my sixteenth birthday and before serving my full enlistment was given an honorable minority discharge. In the summer months I hitch-hiked the highways of the western states and worked at odd jobs, the wheat harvest, truck driving and I roughnecked in the oil fields of North Dakota. One summer, I worked as a cowboy. Later I was drafted into the Army.

I was stationed at Worms on the Rhine River, which was then West Germany. I was attached to a missile battalion – but because of a creative background, I was given a position with the Special Services. I formed my own band, *The Versatile Vagabonds*, and we played pop, rock and country music at various military bases.

Ina wanted to know if I had heard about her and Gene when I was in the orphanage. I told her I had. Others in the family knew about them as well. But we seldom talked about it. It was just another dream to think about. The first film I ever saw was a Gene Autry movie, I told her. It was showing at the Coronado Theatre, two miles away and I crawled under the orphanage fence to go see it. The manager knew where I was from but took pity. He handed me a sack of popcorn, ushered me in free and then, when the movie was over, he drove me back to the hole beneath the fence.

I showed Ina an old picture that had been taken of her years before. She snapped it from my hand and put it away, promising an updated version in return. In the old black and white photo, Ina's front teeth were a little more pronounced than the ones in the beautiful smile before me. I liked her a lot, but for some reason I was never comfortable around her. I felt utterly out of place. There was this quiet apprehension surrounding us that kept me uptight. It gave rise to a vision of me showing up at Ina's place in an old truck like the one in the movie classic, *The Grapes of Wrath.* Of course, even if it were possible, I would never have done it. It was simply a humorous notion, my way of measuring the enormous differences between us. Unlike Ina, I was just a poor Okie.

Occasionally, Gene would pause before me at the doorway of the Continental and tell me to get rid of my uniform hat and jacket. Then we would find a secluded table and have breakfast together. Sometimes Gene and I would go back to the hotel freezer and pick the best steaks we could find for a weekend cookout. It was a fun job, but it didn't pay much, so I quit and went to work during Christmas season for the Hollywood post office. After which, it was Yellow Cab and part-time at Shakey's Pizza on the corner of Orange and Santa Monica Boulevard.

During the same period, I became the Hollywood representative for a company called Parker Arms & Munitions in Orange, California. I sold a new kind of safety blank ammunition to movie studios. The powder used in the Parker blanks was patented. After my demonstration of how safe the blanks were, compared to the standard Remington 5-in-1 blanks and their history of injuries, the Stuntmen of Motion Pictures implored the studios to supply them with Parker ammunition. But, unfortunately, after *The Hollywood Reporter* released the story of the new Parker ammunition, the usual providers of the old ammunition momentarily caught off guard, reasserted a stronger presence. And, completely unaware of how hopeless the situation was, I nevertheless continued trying.

Soon, I was acquainted with many studio guards. I could go in and out of most studios at will. Many times, I stuffed the trunk of my car with actor friends. After being waved through the gate, I would drive to an empty back lot and let them out. Then, they would scatter in all directions, in search of their *Big Break!*

I had a wife Kristine, a son Aaron, and a dream that I had been lugging around as far back as I could remember. It was a thing that no one could take away, give or share.

I could plainly see myself on horseback, beneath a blue sky, in wide-open country. How to do it was not clear, but the time to make it a reality was near. I got some weird looks when I came through the door of my Hollywood apartment at 1822 North Wilton Place with a U.S. Cavalry saddle on my shoulder. I hung the saddle over the back of the couch and no one could comfortably sit there because of it. It was a tiny segment of a dream still yearning to be lived.

One evening, with topographic maps spread over the floor from the living room to the kitchen, Kristine mashed out her cigarette, looked at me and blew out the smoke.

"You're really going to do it, aren't you?" she said.

"I don't know!" I looked at the maps and sipped my coffee.

"You don't, huh? So... the saddle's a new piece of furniture and we're going to be stepping over maps from now on?"

"I don't know if I know what I'm doing," I said. "I just need to be free for a little while. It's not you. I'm getting nowhere."

Kristine exploded. "Dammit! If it's really that important, do it!" There was a long silence and then, with an impetuous smile, she stepped over the maps and put her arms around my neck. "You've never owned a horse. Don't you need one to go with the saddle?" She tickled me and we laughed.

Of course I did need a horse, but at the time, I had no idea where I might get one. And, there was no place to keep a horse, living one block north of Hollywood Boulevard.

"Spivey, you won't get ten miles on a horse. Who do you think you are, Kit Carson?" an actor friend John Donovan said and then laughed like Sidney Greenstreet's in the old classic *The Maltese Falcon* we had watched the night before on TV.

We were with friends on a weekend outing in the hilly desert near Lancaster. It was a great place to shoot, blow off steam and have a good time. Donovan gripped my shoulder and shook me fondly. We walked to the hillcrest and he spread out his arms.

"My friend, look out there. Look at all the damn fences and cars. How do you get from one town to another without becoming road kill, huh? We're thirty miles from LA, but where does it end?"

"I'll stay away from towns," I said. "I'll ride the backcountry. If I can't go around, I'll ride the rail-bed. Nothing blocks the railroad. Hey! I'll cut the damn fences and go where I wanna go. Is this America? Well, I'm an American, damn it." I lowered my voice. "It's all gonna be gone, John."

"It is gone! Long gone, accept it," he said.

"Not all. Then I'll take what's left!"

He laid an arm on my shoulder and we started down the hill.

"I don't get it. We're in Hollywood to make movies. And you want to get on a damned horse and get lost? What's wrong with you? What about Kristine?" We faced one another.

"I'll make my own movie. It'll be real and in my head forever. Anyway, Kris is all for it. Freedom, John! Real freedom, just for a little while."

"Freedom's for the rich!" John sang out. Then, he relented. "Okay! Maybe this poor boy has found a way, huh?" Abruptly, he changed the subject. "Hey! I'll teach you how to shoot that new gun and you can tryout my new Pentax, what do you say?"

John B. Donovan. His camera and my pistol worked out fine. Note the spent 9mm hull above his head.   Jefferson Spivey

I did much of my writing in the cab while waiting for customers. One evening in front of the Roosevelt Hotel, the last cab in line, I wrote down some thoughts to help express why I felt compelled to make such a drastic commitment. As I wrote, my words became sentences.

: Sojourn, search, isolation, solitude. The heady scent of freedom beckons... intimacy of space... to wait is to be too late!

: The cager of animals has at last caged himself. Is there time? Is there room for a lonely quest, an impossible search for a star that was once America? What of America is left? Surely there's a little bit left. Enough to see what they saw, stand where they stood, and touch what they touched? Why attempt it? Better than living at the fringes of a society unable to accept the true individual... unable to cope with only ONE.

Even with these thoughts, I still wondered *why?* Maybe it had something to do with the orphanage where my mother put me at the age of three. That moment framed a picture in my mind that will never lose its vivid colors.

"I'm going to get you some candy at the filling station and I'll be right back," she had said.

The nun who took charge of me was Sister Celine. My fear of her grew into fond memories years later. For the moment, she tried to get my attention by placing a large silver cross in my hand. The cross that was chained to her wide leather belt did not hold my interest very long. As I watched my mother leave, dread set in. I'm not sure how, but I knew my mother would not be coming back. I was too shy to cry, to show any emotion, so I closed my eyes, bowed my head and locked it all inside.

Perhaps my dream to escape on horseback was a reasonable reaction to being confined and constantly regimented when very young. When it was too cold to go out and play, I would sit in the window sill and there, with kids playing all around, I watched squirrels search the playground and the leaves swirl in the wind. I remember thinking – *they're freer than me!* Why? Only by living the dream could I possibly know. At the moment something inside said that it did not matter why, just that I must do it.

After loading six large grocery bags into the back seat of my cab, I opened the front passenger door and helped the elderly woman into the front seat. Then, I went back, slid in, and lowered the flag.

"Eighty cents?" she screeched. "We haven't moved and it's already eighty cents? This is robbery."

"Right," I agreed. "Highway robbery at that."

"Don't get smart. I know your supervisor. That damn meter is off. It was forty cents last week. This is downright stealing from the public."

I held up my hand to silence her.

"I don't set the meter price ma'am, but if you'll tell me where you live, you can call the supervisor when we get there."

"Down the alley over there," she said pointing. I drove in that direction. "It's only two blocks... in the back. The other driver used to pick me up all the time. Why did they send you? He was always here to meet me. He always carries my groceries."

"Yeah well, times change! But don't worry ma'am, I'll carry your groceries." A tear streaked down her cheek.

After lugging the six bulging sacks up the long flight of back-alley stairs, I paused at the door to collect the fare. The woman counted it out on the palm of my hand. Then she added fifty cents for a tip.

"Thanks ma'am." I flipped the half-dollar, caught it, and slapped it on my arm. "Tails. You win!" I put it in her hand and as I started down the stairs, the door slammed behind me. I got in the cab and mopped my face with my shirtsleeve. I wanted her to have the money, but she had taken it as an insult. I entered the ride on my trip sheet, started the engine and drove away.

With coffee to go, I left the Copper Skillet restaurant on Sunset Boulevard just as the streetlights flickered and gradually grew bright. It was time to turn in 3059.

As I approached my cab I noticed an attractive young lady waiting. She looked tired.

"Need a ride?" I said.

"Is this your cab?"

"Sure is." I put on my Yellow Cab hat. "Where to?"

"A hospital," she said. "The problem is I don't have a dime."

I nodded sympathetically and looked to see if anyone was watching. Then, I opened the door and pointed at the back seat.

"Get in and lay down. "

"You mean...right here?"

"What? Oh, no! Just lie down so the supervisor won't see you. If he does, and the roof light's on, he'll know I'm giving a free ride."

I closed the door gently against her sandaled feet, then walked around and got in. I started the engine, turned on the headlights and backed up. Her hands were covering her face and she was quietly sobbing. I headed east on Sunset Boulevard.

"Thank you," she said. "Sorry for what I thought."

"Forget it. General Hospital's the best. Ten minutes!"

After filling the gas tank for the graveyard shift, I gathered up my notebook and waybill. Then, ten minutes late, I held open the cab door for Richard Schmidt, the night driver.

"I'll come in early tomorrow, I promise."

"Okay! There's a note for you at the window," Richard said. "Ina Autry."

"Thanks. Say Rich! Ever hear of Bobbie Bennett?"

"The agent? Sure, she's big. And I don't mean fat."

"She's looking at some of my stuff."

"Very good. But why her, when you've got Gene Autry who owns part of the world?"

"Gene's not in show business anymore."

"Work it man, work it," he growled.

At the turn-in window, I slid my trip-sheet and earnings through a metal slot. The cashier counted the money.

"Fifty-two?" he said, and then handed me a note. "Gene Autry's wife no less. How did you get in with them?"

"She's my cousin."

"And you're driving a cab?"

With a shrug, I walked away.

I dumped my gear in the seat of my '62 Ford and got in. After several failures to start, I got out, lifted the hood and took the cover off the carburetor. I closed the butterfly to stifle the air intake and tried again. The engine quaked into a steady rumble. I slammed the hood and hurried back to keep it running.

Anxious about the call from Ina, I took the Hollywood Freeway and got off at Coldwater Canyon. When I arrived at the Autry home, I parked behind three other cars, Ina's gold Cadillac, Gene's light blue Lincoln, and a white family station wagon.

"I came straight out," I said, when Ina opened the door.

Christmas gifts were stacked everywhere. Gene was in a robe, sitting in his chair and talking on the phone to someone.

"If you can find a place to sit, Jeff, please do." She went up the white-carpeted stairs. Instead of finding a seat, I strolled around. A closet door in the bedroom stood ajar. Several neat rows of hand-tailored boots were visible, all with the *Flying "A"* symbol, wings attached to the letter A just above the slanted boot heels. I paused at the patio window to admire the large empty pool. It was surrounded by tile and billowing flowers. Gold and platinum records covered the wall above the mantle. Though I had seen them before, it was always a new discovery.

The first time I had been in the room, Ina told me a little history of each of the top selling records above the mantle. The most fascinating to me happened during her spring-cleaning of the living room shelves. Stacks of songs, some handwritten by people around the country were taking up too much room.

Ina went through each stack, throwing them away. Many songs had no return addresses and a few lacked even the writer's name. She read one song with a little more interest but also threw it away. Then, she reconsidered. She reached back into the trash and retrieved it. From that decision on, millions of dollars were, and are still, being made. The song that Ina retrieved from the trash can was none other that, *Rudolph the Red-Nosed Reindeer.* On her advice, Gene recorded the song and added another fortune to his already sizable treasure chest.

Gene hung up the telephone and came toward me with his hand out and smiling.

"Hello, Jeff," he said. "Did Audie give back your story?

"Never did." I shrugged. "I still have a copy."

Gene was referring to the actor Audie Murphy. Murphy in the midst of a divorce was also the most decorated soldier in World War II. He was living at the Continental Hotel and was months behind on his rent. The story I had given him was called *The Hawk.* I had written it with a television series in mind. Knowing Audie's situation, I held scant hope for any real development.

"I saw that television spot you did," Gene said. "Did they pay?"

"Yeah, Worthington Dodge. It was a one-shot deal."

"How did you learn to handle a gun like that? He said, then asked as an afterthought, "How's the writing?"

"Okay. I met an agent..."

"Making any headway?"

"Writing yes, selling no. But, I met this agent that might..."

"It's tough," he went on to say. "How would you like a couple of baseball tickets?"

"Baseball? Well, uh... sure."

Ina came forward and handed me a list of names and addresses.

"I guess you've been wondering what this is all about. Well, Christmas is two weeks away, and I wondered if you might help with the strain."

"Sure, what can...?"

"Here's what it is. The station wagon is full of Christmas presents, and that list is where they go. Here's a credit card for gas." Ina put the card in my hand and turned me toward the front door. Just then, Gene came back into the room with a golden gun. He handed it to me.

"Have you ever seen one like this?"

"Never! Beautiful, gold and ivory."

"Can you clean it up?"

"Sure, be happy to. Keep it until I get back." I handed the gun to Ina; she placed it gently on the breakfast bar.

"Jeff, we really appreciate this."

"Don't mention it," I waved and went to my car.

While I waited on a literary agent to sign me up, I continued worked on a novel in my cab. Also, I taught gun handling, two hours a week to actors and would-be actors.

When the call finally came, it turned out to be a disappointment. On my way to the agency my car broke down. Then, after walking from Hollywood to Beverly Hills, the agent was not there. Instead, the secretary pointed to my scripts. They were stacked right where I had placed them a month before. As I thumbed through the material, I realized that not a page had been turned. All the handwritten inserts were exactly as I had left them. The would-be actress/secretary with a telephone clamped to her ear never looked up from arranging glamour photographs of herself. I took the material and left.

The following day, like many times before, I parked my cab on the freeway shoulder near Pomona. My fingers were hooked in the fence of the Kellogg Arabian Horse Ranch. Beyond the fence, horses ran wild. They will never be free, I thought. They're fenced in. I'm fenced out. They have no choice. But I do.

The next day I headed for Burbank, to the International Arabian Horse Association. Without an appointment, I went barging through the front door. Ordinarily, I was not that aggressive but I was desperate and determined to throw off all the controls on my life. Yet, I was fearful, but absolutely ready to beg for the dream.

I spread a map of the American continent over Ralph Goodall's desk. He was the executive secretary and I told him I needed an Arabian horse to accomplish the journey mapped out before him. After dismissing the stone-faced receptionist, Goodall studied the map. He moved his finger along the winding route I had marked. His finger paused and began to tap.

"From Manitou Springs, Colorado, you've got one going north and the other goes east. Which would it be?"

"Probably east, but I figured I'd get to Manitou Springs first, then decide."

Goodall looked out the window, his eyes shifting in thought. Then when he finally spoke, it was as if, to himself.

"Either way, it would be quite a ride."

He peered at me over his horn-rimmed glasses. "Do you really think you can do it?"

"Yes sir. With the right horse I can."

Immediately, he went to work to secure me a horse. He sent out flyers to all those in the association and the waiting began. As I reflect, it seems fantastic that Goodall, a man I had spoken to only once on the phone and a second time in his office, would have that much faith in me, a total stranger. It was bad enough that I lived in Hollywood. Lucky for me, Goodall never thought to ask if I had ever owned a horse before.

I turned my cab off the freeway and my hands tightened on the steering wheel. I was on Vine and down the hill in front of me was Hollywood Boulevard, packed with traffic. The two men in the back seat were well on their way to being drunk. They had insisted upon seeing Hollywood and Vine.

"Here we are," I said.

One loosened his tie and leaned out the window for a better look. Horns blared, and cars were bumper to bumper. The local sport of not letting anyone cross the Boulevard, especially cabs, had become a Saturday night ritual. Even the police would avoid this intersection, where it was nearly impossible to get through.

"Wow, Capitol Records," the man hung out the window and shouted, then he sank back in the seat and sang, "Strangers in the night, la-dee-dee, doo-doo."

"Hey, cabby, take us to the girls. We'd like to do a little recording ourselves."

"And where might that be?" I said, my adrenaline rising.

"Don't bullcrap us, man. Come on, we'll pay."

"You'll have to find your own women." I stepped on the gas, and then hit the brake. The passengers went sliding forward against the back of my seat. "Sorry about that," I lied. "They're not gonna let us through." I put the cab in reverse and backed up quickly. Again, the light turned green, and the narrow space ahead was closing fast. My cab leaped forward on squealing tires and I swerved, but not fast enough. There was an ominous grinding sound and my Checker cab, built like an army tank, left the Chevy classic without a rear bumper guard. The metal guard sent sparks flying before it bounced against the curb and onto the sidewalk. I stopped at the curb, got out and opened the passenger door.

"OUT!"

"You nuts?" The man said as he dug in his pocket.

"Yeah, but not a pimp!" I piled their luggage on the sidewalk.

"Okay, pal. Don't get sore. Will forty bucks..."

"Yeah, just barely." I took the money and pointed. "We just crossed Hollywood and Vine. Now, wasn't that exciting?" I got back in the cab, slammed the door and drove away.

I pulled into the driveway of my apartment on Wilton Place and turned off the engine. It had begun to sprinkle and I just sat there watching raindrops merge and streak like silent cracks in the glass of the window. I did not want to go inside yet. I needed to calm down. I loved rain, but at the moment, it was not very uplifting. I felt like I was in a large barrel with the lid closing slowly. There was no way out and no way to stop it from closing. I got out and shut the door quietly. I looked up at the warm yellow light in the window and thumped my cigarette into the gutter. Then, I took a deep breath of cleaned air, and started up the stairs.

Kristine opened the door with a surprised smile. "Ili Jeff. Something wrong?"

"Nah, I just turned in early. Any coffee?"

"I'll make some. But first," she said mysteriously, hiding something behind her back, "Robert Kennedy's going to be at the Greek Theatre tomorrow in Griffith Park. Can we go?"

"Sure," I smiled and shrugged. "Who in the world can stop us?"

"Great! Here." She gave me a slip of paper. "Ralph Goodall. He found you a horse! I think. You're supposed to call that number."

"Really?" I looked at the note. "Abbeville, South Carolina?"

"Yes! A Dr. Rosenberg. He owns an Arabian horse farm."

"I can't believe it!" We stood in utter silence. Everything had already been said. We both looked over at Aaron. He was asleep, and the tiny radio in his crib quietly played Antonio Carlos Jobim's *Black Orpheus*. It was sad, our lives were about to change. Then, I remembered Deborah, Kristine's sister. She would be moving in and Aaron would get more love from them both than any Spivey kid should be allowed to have. The thought made me feel better, but the fear of what lay ahead quickly took over.

I went to the back porch to look and listen to the rain and to think. The leaves of the avocado tree, dripping with water, reflected a fiery glow from the porch light. *We won't be giving avocados to the neighbors any more,* I thought. But, I knew they would get them anyway. I felt the proverbial butterflies in my stomach. It was truly the time to put-up or shut-up. But, I had not the slightest inclination of turning back.

I heard the telephone ring and then the back door opened and Kristine handed me a cup of coffee.

"It's long distance. Rosenberg!" She said.

With phone in hand, I sank down beside my saddle, took a sip of coffee and said in a clear voice, "Jefferson Spivey here!"

It was Edith Rosenberg. As she spoke I looked at Kristine. She was standing in the kitchen doorway solemnly smiling. I reached for the stirrup of my saddle and traced the deep imprint of U S stamped in the leather with my finger. "How soon?" I asked, "Uh, how 'bout early April?" I hung up and gawked at Kristine. "Can you believe it? They're sending me a horse named Mr. Sol! All the way from South Carolina."

Ralph Goodall took the first ride on Mr. Sol and my saddle. *js*

21

Two weeks out. California and more desert ahead. *js*

The Desert

I awoke with a start. My horse was nudging my shoulder with his nose. The pain in my stomach was gone. Using a dangling stirrup, I tugged myself to a sitting position. There was a sudden loud boom. Then, I remembered seeing the surrounding area on the map that had blown away. I was on or near a military target range.

It was evening. I had slept all day, and the thought of losing so much time was distressing. I retrieved the Colt from the sand. The loading-gate was still open. I chambered a new round, holstered the gun and I got to my feet. I lifted the waterbag to the saddle, took a wrap on the reins and mounted the long swell of land ahead.

I paused at the crest before a vast panorama of earth and sky. It was sundown, and the last golden shafts of light streaked out a brilliant deep violet to touch my horse and me. A familiar sound brought a sigh of relief when I saw headlights probing the lowland darkness miles north. At that moment, I knew we had made it.

On the map, the region was called Devil's Playground. I took a canvas bucket from the saddle and with Sol fighting me for a drink I filled it. As he sucked up the water, I looped the waterbag straps over the pommel of the saddle and drank from the spigot.

"We did it, Sol." Feeling grateful, with Sol slobbering beside me, the metal bit clattering in his mouth, I wanted to do something really charitable. I took the bit from his mouth and bridle from his head. And then, though it was the best of leather and garnished with silver beads, I threw it away. Then, I slipped the reins through the rings of the halter and gave Sol a pat. "That better?"

We started out again. It was getting dark and desert shadows were on the move. I felt the presence of something behind us and I thought of the mule. I looked back, but nothing was there. I shortened the reins and with that old feeling of guilt, we went on, my spurs and Sol's hooves grinding softly in the silence.

We were somewhere west of Afton Canyon, California, following the high railbed when we entered a cut. It rose so gradually on both sides that I hardly even noticed. The cut was just wide enough on one side to ride. The other side was too narrow for us to pass without scraping my right stirrup against the wall. We stayed to the left, and entered the mile long cut beneath a beautiful primrose sky. Far ahead beyond the end of the cut I noticed a semaphore just as it turned from red to green.

"What the heck does that mean?" I grumbled, thinking how stupid it was to have a red and green light switching on and off in the middle of nowhere. Sol jerked suddenly to the left, his neck bowed and his muzzle pulled in. With his head turned and his ears listening, he started a sidestepping prance. "What is it?" Just as I asked, I realized what it was. Even astride Sol's back I heard a deep thumping hum, quickly growing louder.

"A train? TRAIN'S COMIN'!"

Which way? I reined Sol this way and that, but the only way out was straight ahead. I rolled my spurs against his trembling hide and Sol leaped into a powerful run. The gravel of the railbed shot like bullets from his pounding hooves. Sol continued shying to the left, trying to avoid the clattering drone of iron wheels vibrating the railbed under foot. I looked back; the train was coming eighty miles an hour. There was no escape.

I drew Sol to a gravel-spraying halt. We spun around and I backed him against the wall. He would not stand with his side against the cut. Instead, he faced the tracks. "Oh no!" I groaned. I had thrown the bridle and bit away! With one arm around his neck, I stroked him hard with clawing fingers. His head was so high and far back, his mane was in my face.

"Good boy! It's okay!" I tried to keep my voice calm, to hide my own fear. The train grew larger and louder, as it raced toward us.

Sol began to quake. I kept speaking in his ear. The train blared out as it thundered by, two feet in front of us. Sol jerked suddenly forward; He was confused. Rocks poured from the wall behind us and pounded his rump. I thought he might bolt into the train. I had no real control. All I could do was hold tight and keep talking.

I thought the mile long train would never end. Finally and abruptly, it did and my arms grew even tighter around his neck. "You're a good boy, Sol." I dismounted. Sol was sitting on the ground against the wall; his tail tucked under him like a dog.

I tugged the reins and he straightened up on all fours, blowing loud and listening to the hum of the tracks. I shook my fist as it faded. "You missed, you... " But then, I reconsidered and looked skyward. "Thanks!" We started out. "You know, Sol, sometime we should stop long enough to get acquainted."

At the end of the cut, we went down the sloping railbed and headed north toward a tiny oasis in the distant flats.

A wave of soft wind brushed over the campfire. I lay looking up, with my head in the slope of the saddle. The sky was filled with a billion stars, a sight I could not remember having seen before. My dapple-gray gelding turned in the moonlight with his head high and ears pointing. He was listening to something far off. It was like seeing him for the first time and it made me whisper.

"Wow. Lucky me."

A deadly little snake appeared suddenly and silently in the firelight. I drew back the hammer of my .45, as the sidewinder rattlesnake looped out its coils twice more to get closer. The snake raised its head and tested the air with its tongue. My Colt was loaded with cut-down .410 shotgun shells. It would have been a simple matter to blow the snake to bits. However, there was no earthly reason to do so. The snake had not come to attack me, and after all, I was the intruder. It occurred to me; the snake may have never seen a man or fire before. I eased down the hammer of my gun, and with a stick, I carried the creature far out into the darkness and tossed it into a sandy ravine. After stacking my gear around the slope of the saddle, I held my hands closer to the dwindling firelight to examine the deep red cracks on my knuckles. Then, in the great silence I went to sleep wishing for that bottle of Cornhuskers lotion that I had thrown away.

It was the last town in California. I came upon sign that read 'Population 3.' But upon closer examination, I could see that it had been 30. Someone had covered the zero with matching white paint, leaving only the three showing. Maybe twenty-seven people moved away, I thought, as I rode on with the morning sun in my face. Perhaps the three who stayed couldn't afford a new sign.

When I reached the tiny settlement, I dismounted before a café that actually had a hitching rack. The place was real enough, but it looked like a Hollywood set. The day was warm and quiet. I stepped to the boardwalk with a hollow thump. My spurs rang and my gaze shifted like a man ready to draw his gun on the slightest move. It was fun. If someone was watching from inside, I hoped they were whispering to one another.

I paused at the door, pulled down my hat, and tightened the chinstrap. With a straight face, I pushed the door inward and looked into the eyes of a short, fat woman, who was wiping a glass. Her red cheeks grew even redder when she smiled. An old man was crouched down across the room. He was scrubbing the wooden floor near a fireplace. There was one other man sitting at the end of the bar holding a cup of coffee. As the three of them looked me over, I rested my hand on the butt of my Colt. And, assuming they had seen the movie *Shane,* instead of the menacing use of gloves, I took another step forward and said, accusingly, "So! You're the three!"

In the thoughtful silence, eyes shifted back and forth. Then my question and demeanor was understood. Laughter filled the room.

"You should be an actor."

"Think so? Heck! And I just left Hollywood."

Thanks to the *three*, I got my first cafe-cooked breakfast since the journey began. I was able to clean up a bit, rearrange my gear, and refill my canteen with some good tasting water. Then, before leaving, I used a pay phone to call home. The phone, sandblasted by the hot desert wind, was bolted to a wooden light pole in an empty lot of rocks and cactus next to the cafe. The only shade was under the brim of my hat.

Kristine and Aaron were doing fine. She had quit her bank job and would be working at a Hollywood bookstore on Fairfax, she said. I told her not to worry and before we hung up, she told me that Ina Autry had called. Gene wanted to thank me for a *fine* job cleaning his ivory-handled, gold-plated Colt. And my good buddy, John Donovan had put up a hundred dollar bet that I would never make it out of California.

"You can tell Donovan he just lost a hundred bucks...tomorrow morning I'll be in Nevada. If you want, drop me a card at General Delivery, Boulder City, Nevada. Okay?"

Trekking through the El Dorado Mountains of Nevada, I came upon the fresh diggings of an old mine. Halfway around the foothills was the miner himself. We quickly became friends. He was an old gentleman who introduced himself as Ed. He lived in a small house trailer with a blue canvas awning above the door.

Ed was cooking over an open fire. Thor, a German shepherd with about half an ear torn off from a fight with coyotes, fetched rocks instead of sticks. Thor fell in love with my horse. The gray and black shepherd followed my horse everywhere he went, from one grassy clump to another.

"Better tie him up before I leave in the morning," I warned.

"I've had that dog since he was a pup. He'd never leave this place." Ed handed me a plate with two thick steaks heaped with mashed potatoes and venison gravy.

"Thanks." I took the pot from the fire, leaned to one side and filled my cup. I sensed that the old man did not want to talk about his years of mining. He'd been working his claim for the past six years, sometimes lucky, sometimes not. "Guess it gets lonely out here. Do you ever have visitors?"

"Being lonely or alone is not necessarily bad. I love being alone. It makes for other things." He flipped his steak bone into the air and Thor's teeth snapped loud in the darkness. Ed leaned forward and fanned gnats from his coffee cup. From where we sat we could see the glow of Boulder City, straight north. "I've got a brother in San Francisco who can't stand to be alone," he said. "People like that have got problems. He was just here, trying to get me to go back."

"Back to the big city, huh?"

"Yes. Back to being a lawyer."

"Really?"

"We both were. He still is, got it all! Money, wife, kids… Drives one of those big'ol Mercedes Benzes. The whole bit. His forty-year-old son had a stroke. They stuck pins in his jaw, and he couldn't feel it." He looked over at his dog. Thor paused his grinding on a bone, got up and came closer. Ed gave him a gentle pat. "If you hadn't ridden up here on a horse, I wouldn't be telling you all this."

"Yeah, well, you can't roll up a window on a horse."

"Haw, I like that." He sniffed. "That's it."

"Have you got it in for attorneys or your brother?"

"Both. Never liked either."

"He must care about you if he came to get you."

"No. Guilt brought him here." He poured his coffee into the fire, stood up and looked toward Boulder City. "How long will it take to ride thirty-two miles?"

"Most of the day," I told him. "We'll get an early start, while it's dark and cool."

"You could stay a day or two."

"I appreciate the offer, but I'd better keep going."

"Sure. I understand. By the way that brother of mine, it's a story better left untold." He started for his trailer. "We'll have coffee before you leave. Good night."

"Night!" I walked over to the water barrel, lifted the wooden lid and filled the dipper twice. It was wonderful to have good water. When the trailer light went out, I hung the dipper and went for my sleeping bag. As I lay back, Thor settled between Sol and me. Occasionally, the big dog raised his head and pointed his one ear in the direction of a yelping pack of coyotes. He made an attempt to howl, then rolled on his side and looked up at Sol.

I opened my eyes just as Ed walked past me with a bucket of water. He sat it in front of Sol and then went back to bed.

The next time I opened my eyes, it was dawn and Ed was waiting by the fire with a pot of boiled coffee.

With Sol saddled and cinched up, I swung the belted gun around my waist and buckled it. I crouched down, refilled the porcelain cup, took one of the biscuits Ed had fried in the skillet and the two of us sat watching the gray fog dissipate above the yellow flames.

"When I woke up," I said, breaking the silence. "I was thinking about people like us, who are... well…"

"Loners?"

"Yeah! I like people alright, but I guess I'm a hermit at heart."

"It starts early," Ed said. "When you're severely mistreated by the ones you love and trust." I shot him a glance. I knew he was talking about himself but, in just one sentence he had exposed a collection of bad memories I had locked away. He smiled. "It's a tougher row to hoe! But that easy life's not worth a plug nickel."

I got to my feet. The lights of Boulder City were fading. I finished my biscuit and coffee and changed the subject.

"Thanks for watering my horse last night."

"You're welcome. When you get to Boulder, maybe you should see a doctor. A little checkup, you know?"

"Yeah, maybe a vet to look at my horse."

"Yes. Lose him, you lose your freedom."

"That's true!"

"Do you always wear the gun?"

"Most of the time. Sometimes I let my horse carry it." I grinned.

"You should have been here a couple of days ago. They were shooting at my trailer from the highway. You know… potheads? They think I'm crazy." He followed me to my horse. "Probably good you weren't here."

"Maybe you should get a gun. What about the law?"

"What can they do? Me! Way out here?"

"There's no justice if you don't get it."

"Oh yes, law and justice. There's no correlation between the two, but I know what you mean." Ed smiled and we shook hands.

"Thanks for everything." I mounted, rattled a spur and Sol stepped out. "See you next spring."

Two miles into the flats Sol jumped fearfully and I nearly came out of the saddle from the onrush of a one-eared dog. Thor dashed ahead of us with his tongue dripping. I fired my gun to scare him but he ran ahead, joining in on what he thought was a hunt.

"Man's best friend? Haw!"

In Boulder City, Margaret Richardson, who wrote for the *Las Vegas Review Journal*, bought me supper and did a story. That evening I borrowed a pickup and took Thor back home. I called out a few times, but Ed was not around. Perhaps he was on his way to Boulder City to find the dog he believed would never leave him. I tied Thor to the trailer and drove away, promising myself that I would someday see them both again.

Kristine's postcard was cheerful enough, but the inferences of her words revealed a bad standing for me. After a lonesome night in a hay-barn, Sol and I headed for Indian country.

In Boulder City, Thor fetched a rock for the reporter. 🐾 Irene J. Brennan/ R-J

Canyon Country

On a ragged asphalt road winding into the empty distance, we came to a wide drainage ditch, a natural cut in the land where the road curved and narrowed on either side with no shoulders or curb. I dismounted, took a wrap on the reins and walked on.

It was late noon, beautiful and quiet. The Nevada desert was in full bloom and the sun was beginning to glare in my face. The sound of an approaching automobile joined the grinding of our footsteps. I shortened the reins, moved to the edge of the road and looked into the drainage ditch fifteen feet down. At that moment an old pickup coming in a cloud of dust swerved dangerously close, and as it passed, there was a loud backfire. Sol threw his head back and reared. I thought he would back off the edge of the road, but I pulled him down.

"Drunken idiot!" I stopped walking and turned my head to listen. The sound of the pickup faded in the distance.

That backfire could have been an accident I rationalized as we continued. Just then, the sound of the engine was there again and growing louder.

"DAMN!"

We were at the apex of the curve and above the deepest part of the ditch. I led Sol to the edge of the road, shortened the reins, backed up against him and waited.

The headlights flashed into view behind us.

This man was playing dangerously. I drew my gun, cocked back the hammer, and held it pointed straight down. The engine revved to its peak and backfired again. The tires hit a patch of asphalt and the old Ford swerved toward the drop-off. The driver regained control and just as the pickup hurtled by, I raised the gun and fired. A hot, pungent air exploded from the tire and stung my face with dirt and debris.

Momentarily blinded and spitting dirt, I fought to control my frightened horse. Then I watched as the pickup bounded off the road and bounced to a halt in a cloud of dust thirty yards into the prairie. I holstered my gun, hooked the hammer-tie, and swung to the saddle.

I started to ride out and confront the man but changed my mind. He had climbed into the bed of his pickup. His long black hair whipped as he shook his head back and forth. It looked like he might be waiting, maybe with a shotgun. I chose not to find out. Instead, I called out cheerfully.

"Boy, those backfires are hell on tires!"

I left the road and headed north for open country. As the air grew cold and the sun moved down in the west, painting the sky with gold and pastels, I found a corner section of an old dwelling and there I camped for the night. I tied Sol so that I could see him through the open window. Then, I went to sleep thinking how under different circumstances the driver of the pickup and I might have been friends and how I would remember that bizarre encounter forever. And perhaps, the stranger would remember too.

It looked like a day's ride, but it was two. Out of a cold Nevada wind. 📷 *js*

Peach Springs is a small sunbaked settlement on the Hualapai Indian reservation in Arizona. Here Sol received his first set of shoes since leaving California. A wonderful old Indian wearing a heavy plaid shirt and a battered cowboy hat took off the old shoes. Then, he led Sol to a shady spot in his small corral and without a word saddled his horse and rode off to the general store in Peach

Springs. He returned at noon with cold drinks, a heavy sack lunch, and a new set of horseshoes that he nailed to Sol's hooves.

Beyond Peach Springs, Sol and I took to the backcountry. In three days we reached the South Rim of the Grand Canyon.

"Look, Sol. This all happened about three million years before we got here."

I slipped from the saddle. Standing on a rock face, I saw why this beautiful place was considered one of the great wonders of the world. As I studied the monumental rip, I questioned the theory that the rushing waters of the Colorado River solely created it. I wondered, couldn't the riverbed have already been laid by a cataclysmic fault in the earth's crust? And if not, why hadn't the enormous onslaught of water, instead of cutting through seemingly solid rock, taken a more southerly route over softer earth?

Logbook: May 18, Grand Canyon.

Yesterday, State Senator Sam McConnell, representing Governor Jack Williams came to meet me. We stood for news photos, with tourists looking on. McConnell asked me if I needed anything. Should have told him, "Hand lotion," but I didn't. After Sol and I had our picture made with Betty Verkamp and her ten-week-old daughter Kelly Ann in front of Verkamp's Indian Handcraft & Souvenirs, I rode on to Desert View. I filled my canteen and just as I was about to mount up three young women drove up in a VW bus and parked thirty feet away. They all waved and one of them, an attractive blond, turned up the radio volume and the song, *If you're going to San Francisco* grew louder as the door opened and she stepped down to the asphalt. With the others coaxing her on and with the sun in her face, she began a clownish, attention getting dance, slowly in my direction. Suddenly, in a graceful pose, with her flaxen hair swirling over her shoulder, she stopped.

"Who are you?" she said, "God?"

"No, but He's gotta be near," I replied.

"Claudie, come on!"

With hands raised, she backed away. They drove off, with Claudie thoughtfully staring at Sol and me. Heck! A beauty to behold, I remembered thinking. But, that was yesterday. This is today and the sun's going down. Found a great campsite next to a pond. I'll finish my coffee, check on Sol, wash up and go to bed.

Joe shoed Sol, first set since ride began.

The Grand Canyon.

Holding Kelly Ann Verkamp.

Water! A good place to camp. *js*

The sign read Tsegi, two miles. A dust cloud moved slowly across the road ahead. Indian shepherds were herding several hundred sheep into a ravine. I nudged the gray and continued in the white dust. Two Indian boys looked back at me and paused.

"Hidy!" I said, pressing my fingers to my dry, painful lips. "All those sheep belong to you guys?"

The two boys smiled at one another, and then the older one stepped closer and asked, "Are you Billy the Kid?"

"Fraid not."

"You a cowboy?"

"Yeah. But, no cows." They laughed and I asked, "Is there food at the trading post?"

"Sure. They have hamburgers and everything."

"Great." I readjusted my hat. "How do you say it?"

"The trading post? Tsegi, without the T."

"Segi, huh? You're pretty smart."

"We go to school. We're not dumb." They grinned at each other.

"I didn't mean... Where is the school?"

"It's back that way," he pointed. "You passed it this morning."

"Really?"

"Yeah. Everyone knows you're here."

"Who's everyone?"

"The whole reservation. Are you fast on the draw?"

"Well... I get by." I drew the gun. "Here, take a look."

He took the gun and looked up in surprise.

"It's heavy."

"It's loaded. Be careful."

He gave it back and I twirled it into the holster. The two smiled wide-eyed at one another.

"You're good with that. Do it again."

Considering that they had never seen such a live performance, I spun the gun into the air and caught it by its butt. Then again, I twirled it back into the holster.

"Wow!" They slapped each other on the shoulder and laughed in amazement. "You should do that at the school. They called you Billy the Kid."

"Too far back."

"Will you sleep at the trading post tonight?"

"Yeah. Maybe so. Plenty of water?"

"Sure. There's a faucet, and the canyon where the sheep are going has a stream. It runs behind the trading post."

"Sounds like a good place to camp. Maybe I'll see you there." I nudged Sol and the boys watched as I rode away.

By the time we had covered the last dusty mile to the trading post, it was late noon. Teams of horses and wagons were parked on the northeast corner. I dismounted. Several saddle horses were tied to a hitching rack against the building of pastel red adobe. Women and children watched curiously as I led Sol between the wagons and tied him to a pole. Several horsemen appeared in the doorway and others crowded behind them for a closer look. Most were wearing boots and spurs, pointed-brim hats and bright bandannas.

When I entered, the proprietor, a short, stoutly built, red bearded man was deeply engrossed in a stack of receipts beside the cash register. At least, he pretended to be. He wore a squash-blossom tie and the stubby fingers of his small rugged hands were embellished with silver and turquoise rings. I paused at the counter, and while I waited, I searched the shelves on the back wall. At last, the small blue eyes shifted in my direction.

"What can I do for ya?" he snapped.

"Hi. Do you have any salve, like Vaseline, or lotion that would be good for dry skin?"

"No. We don't carry hand lotion here." None of the onlookers were smiling. Then, he lifted the pocket flap of his khaki shirt and tapped a small badge. "If I was you, young fella, I'd get that gun off and not wear it around here. Now I don't have any jurisdiction on the reservation... but some of these young Navajo police will take you in without even thinkin'."

Over the one thousand miles behind me, I had talked with police, county sheriffs, and camped on Navajo Chief Goldtooth's property. This was the first objection to my wearing a gun.

"Okay. I don't mind. I didn't want to leave it hanging on my saddle."

"If you're worried, the Indians ain't gonna take it," he said so all could hear. "It's the damn whites you gotta worry about."

"You know?" I cut in to say, "I think you're right."

"The Indians here are good folks. They don't steal nothin' round here."

"Well, that's good to know." I rolled the belt around the gun and knife and laid them on the counter. "How's that?"

"No need to be smart about it. The reservation police won't even talk to you; they'll take you right in."

Amidst this communication barrier, I pointed toward the wall shelves. "What's that? The small bottle by itself there?"

"The pink one?"

"Yeah, the pink one."

"That's baby lotion."

"Hey! That's just what I need," I said peering steadily into his tiny blue eyes. "And a can of Spam."

I opened the cooler and took out a carton of milk. I set it beside the baby lotion and Spam. When I pushed my hand into the tight pocket of my Levi's and pulled out a five-dollar bill, blood seeped from the cracked skin of my knuckles.

"You got a little blood leakin' there."

"Yeah, pretty dry." I took the change, and with my holstered gun in one hand, the baby lotion, Spam, and milk in the other, I started for the door.

"There's a faucet by the water tank. You're welcome to use it."

"Thanks!" As soon as the screen door closed, it reopened. It was the proprietor.

"What's your name?" he asked. I turned back and we paused face to face in the shade of an archway.

"Jefferson Spivey. Jeff's fine."

"Good name. Glad to meet you, Jeff. We got started off a little wrong there, but I can tell you're not the showoff I thought you'd be. I'm Jim Porter. Trader Jim, folks call me. There's a shade tree over by the water tank. Plenty of water if you want to clean up and take a rest."

"Well, thanks again. I appreciate it."

"Go on, take it easy," he said backing away. "Maybe we can talk later. There's some hay for that little Appie' right by the fence."

An hour later the sun was blazing in the west. Trader Jim stood a few feet away. He was leaning comfortably against a large wagon wheel. I had not noticed before, but the hair of his beard was predominantly white, not as red as I had thought. He had been telling me some of the more exciting episodes of his life. I spoke up in a moment of silence.

"It's hard to imagine."

"Gettin' shot?"

"No. Well… that too. But mostly, that you actually rode with Pancho Villa. You must have been pretty young."

"I'm seventy-eight. It was Villa's last campaign… 1916, in a town called Torreon. We all were young. I was just thirteen."

"So you got bullets in your legs, and Villa got a ranch."

"Then you know somethin' about it?"

"Actually, I'm about half finished with a novel that takes place in Texas and Mexico at about the same time."

"Wonderful. What's it called?"

"The Law and The Eagle."

"Good title. Do you plan to write about this?"

"I don't know. I keep a logbook just in case."

The door of the trading post opened and banged shut. Several Indians on the way to their saddled horses looked in our direction. Trader Jim called out something in Navajo. He waved, so I assumed he was telling them good night. They all mounted up and reined their horses along the stream. The beige canyon walls blossomed with their colorful dress in the final rays of sunlight. The wagons followed, loaded with children, and flanked by a half dozen dogs, silently trotted along. Soon the trading post was nearly deserted and the grinding of wagon wheels faded.

"Their comin' in now in brand new pickups," Jim said, with an incredulous look on his sunburned face. "In a couple of years ever damn one of them will have a brand new pickup truck." He nodded toward the canyon pass. "Sights like we just saw are gonna be gone forever."

"Where do they get the money?"

"Government!"

"Well! It's long in coming I'd say."

"Yeah, but they don't know what to do with it. They'll go buy a new pickup, fill it with kids and dogs, get drunk, have a wreck and kill 'em all." He wiped his palms over his turquoise rings and went on. "The way I see it, my great-grandfather may have been responsible for some of the bad things done to the Indians, but I'm not. What did I ever do? I help 'em. They're doin' better than a lot of whites, I can tell ya that."

"Whites seem to have a built-in drive to conquer everything. The Indians aren't like that. No need to conquer what you already have, right?" I waited for a response, but none came.

I got to my feet and he followed me over to examine my horse. Sol was contentedly munching hay.

"He looks good, havin' come so far."

"Not bad," I agreed. "By the way, he's an Arabian."

"No foolin'. I thought he was Appaloosa. He's spotted like one."

"Dapple-gray, some call it."

"Shows you what I know. Well, you can sleep out here or under roof. It's your choice."

"Out here's fine."

At that moment an image appeared from out of the shadows. An Indian woman paused before me. She was breathtaking. She wore a deerskin dress, moccasins and a necklace heavy with elk teeth. Feathers were laced in her long braids. Her dark eyes searched my face. She pointed at me and slipped her fingers down one feather. She closed her eyes and uttered something in her own language. She drew in a deep breath and blew it out slowly. Then, she looked at me again and turned away. That was it. She was gone and I looked over at Trader Jim.

"What was that about?"

"She's a Brujo," he said. "An outcast. Still livin' in the past."

"Huh! I wonder what she said?"

"She called you, Binna Du' Duen'o'na'. She said she knew you were comin'."

"What does it mean?"

"It means, Wind Drinker."

"Wind Drinker?"

It's part of the Zuni prayer. It goes... I inhale the warm breath of wind into my system and add to your breath of wind."

"She said that to me?"

"It's very old. You are your own visible spirit."

"Wow! Then, where am I?" I smiled too wide and cracked my chapped lips.

"Well, there's more to it, and I don't know half of it. It's sorta like there's two of you. One's ancient and one's now, each givin' purpose to the other. A Wind Drinker connects the physical to the spiritual universe. It's a special recognition. She honored you."

"Huh. Sorry! I was never into spirits and superstitions," I said, blotting my mouth. Trader Jim peered at me thoughtfully.

"Okay. But don't treat it too lightly," he said. "It's a rare thing and you should take note. Out here, spirits and superstitions are the nitty-gritty's of life. I get up early. See ya in the mornin'."

"Good night."

It was early and I was watering Sol when a man in an old rusty pickup came to fetch me. Boy what a ride that was. It was like riding a wagon with a motor. Milton Roberts, the principal of Red Lake Day School had sent him. The students who had heard about me were anxiously waiting.

By the time we got there, they had put up a corner stage at the end of the dining room. It was the largest room in the school.

I gave a talk and performed gun tricks for the children. I had a great time. Before I left, the good folks there stuffed my backpack with oranges and sandwiches.

Just as the driver and I started for the pickup to leave, all the children dashed from the school, surrounded us, and cheered.

"They all want to go with you, Jefferson," Roberts said as we shook hands and said goodbye.

Back at the trading post, Trader Jim talked me into staying another day. He, along with an assistant, Jimmy Nighthawk, took me on a tour of the reservation. We traveled the full length of Sacred Mountain. Then, by using a newly cut road, we went past work trailers and several earthmovers on our way to the summit.

"Pretty soon," Trader Jim said as we reached the stop, "they're gonna bring in these gigantic super-shovels. Just one shovel, mind you, will hold ten cars."

Atop the massive sanctuary, I felt a little gloomy knowing that ancient ceremonial grounds would soon be destroyed for something far more tangible than mythical shadows of the past. We crossed a couple of dry streambeds and then Trader Jim parked the four-wheel drive. He pointed in all directions and explained how the water from the Colorado River had been diverted, and why.

"For washin' cars in LA," he said. "The streams are gone, and hundreds of sheep and livestock are dyin'."

Trader Jim found a pathway and climbed slowly, huffing and puffing to the top of the highest boulder. He took off his hat and threw it to the ground in front of us. Then, with his head back and his arms stretched toward the flaming red sky, he began shouting in Navajo, loud and clear. I glanced at Nighthawk a couple of times. He appeared uncomfortable, looking up, down, this way and that. I could tell he had seen it all before. Finally, his dark blue eyes paused on me.

"A plea for clouds with water," he said.

On our way back to Tsegi we sipped strong coffee and watched the towering buttes pass.

Trader Jim pointed a stubby finger north. "We're on the Hopi Reservation. Way over there is Monument Valley. The Navajo Reservation surrounds the three Hopi mesas and around that is the State of Arizona. Two states within a state, with their own laws and customs. It's been goin' on since prehistoric man. The Indians are in a big struggle. It's between the old folks, the long hairs who live under the blanket, and the new generation that knows about clean clothes and stereos, eight tracks and havin' babies in hospitals."

"Heck," Nighthawk said, with a lift of his chin. "I have a horse and a pickup too. A true transitional," he said it without laughing, so I kept a straight face.

"What's the big struggle?" I asked.

The young ones are takin' up white man ways. You saw Sacred Mountain, the worshipping grounds are bein' destroyed."

I looked at Nighthawk. His gaze remained on the winding road ahead.

"Are you Navajo, Jimmy?" I asked.

"Ute. Half."

"His father's white," Trader Jim said. "Jimmy's never met him. His mother lives in Albuquerque."

"Well!" Nighthawk shrugged and looked at me, "at least we know he had blue eyes. You have Indian blood?"

"What? Well, uh," I stammered. "Maybe… a little!"

Nighthawk had said it with certainty and had caught me off guard. All I could think of was my mother's words, when at the age of thirteen I had asked her the same question, and she replied. "Don't ever tell anyone you have Indian blood in you." "Why?" I asked. "Just don't!" She said, her dark eyes peering into mine.

"The damn whites contaminate everything don't they?" Trader Jim said bitterly and waited for my reply.

"Well, it's too late now. We are what we are."

An hour later we were back at Tsegi, sitting at a rustic wooden booth. It was then that I brought up a subject that had bothered me since leaving the Grand Canyon.

"Maybe you already know about this," I began, "but a few days ago I was in a basin, a tributary of the Grand Canyon. I heard a roar that sounded like gunfire. I didn't think much about it, they use the Mojave for a testing range, and I figured it was something like that. Later, a helicopter went skimming along the ridge. Well, the day I left the Canyon I met this guy named Jack. He said he worked for the Park and told me that the helicopter, using a machine gun, wiped out a herd of burros!"

"Yeah, the Park Service offered to let the Indians go down and round up the burros," Trader Jim said.

"Why?"

"Food! Burro is good as venison. Anyway, the Indians have no way of rounding them up. Can you imagine trying to round up a herd of deer? That's what it would be like. So they just wipe 'em out. The canyon is the natural habitat of the bighorn sheep. The burros have grown so numerous the bighorn can't survive.

"Must be a lot of burros."

"In the early days the prospector used as many as twenty. When their grubstake ran out, they'd eat 'em, or turn 'em loose. They multiply like deer, ya know."

"You think the bighorn will ever come back?"

"Maybe," Nighthawk said. "But by then, be too many humans. I doubt if they'll wipe *them* out."

"They could have sent trucks to get all that meat," Trader Jim said. "But, we've got enough problems around here. I'll be callin' Goldwater in the mornin' to let him know."

"Senator Barry Goldwater?"

"You damn right!"

Suddenly a Greyhound bus came to a spewing halt just beyond the front door.

"Oh, Boy!" Trader Jim said wringing his hands. "Time to make money!" He hurried away. I went to check on my horse.

Trader Jim, a mystic, I had come to realize proclaimed that *spiritual manipulators* had planned my journey.

Near sundown, he took me into his home behind the trading post. After meeting his wife Carolyn, he opened the jammed door of his living room, flattened out a rug and ushered me through. Wow! A Pharaoh's tomb, I thought. A dusty shaft of sunlight coming through an elongated window lightened the dark corner beyond where silver pots, candleholders, and other objects of antiquity were stacked. Hand woven blankets were high against the north wall. Leather belts heavy with silver Conchos billowed with reams of coral and turquoise beads from varnished rafters. War bonnets, beaded moccasins, bear and wolf hides were spread over the couch and wooden floor. It was all crammed together in one room: all proceeds of toil and dreams from a more illustrious time gone by.

He gave me old postcards of himself with the Trading Post Tsegi in the background. Then, he dug around in a large vase of Indian jewelry and found what he was looking for. It was a ring and he presented it to me. His small blue eyes blinked and grew watery as he pushed it gently over the cracked skin of my knuckle.

"To keep your journey true, a silver ring, an amulet for Wind Drinker and you."

A Council Ring, he called it. The turquoise stone centering the crown was surrounded by ten more and all were different shades.

That night, atop the bluff across the road from Tsegi, I camped in a deserted hogan. Before I turned in, I took off the ring, tied it in a corner of my bandanna and put it in the saddlebag. I disliked wearing jewelry but I wanted to keep the gift in a safe place.

After soaking my hands with the baby lotion, I lay there on the dirt floor of the primitive hogan and watched the small fire I had built. I kept thinking about the outcast Zuni and Trader Jim's translation of what she had said. *Wind Drinker. It's sorta like there's two of you.* Then, as the last tiny flame went out, it dawned on me. Something I never spoke of and almost never thought about. I had been born an identical twin. A *twinless twin* is the term coined for those like me. My twin brother had not survived a premature birth. I went to sleep glad that I had not brought it up. Trader Jim would have had a great time trying to connect all the loose threads in his tangled web of myth.

The next morning, in the dawn's amber light, I saddled my dapple gray and mounted up. With Tsegi still in the valley darkness below, we struck out across the reservation. By starting out early I figured I could at least make it to the San Juan River and perhaps to Yellow Mountain not far beyond. Water was almost always the determining factor for the destination ahead.

On the Reservation. Performing for the children at Red Lake Day School. 🎥 *js*

Old postcard of Tsegi and *Trader* Jim Porter with deputy badge. ⟨⟩ Petley Studios

I halted Sol on the edge of a deep ravine. The land looked the same as far as I could see in both directions. I slipped from the saddle and walked closer. The ravine was fifteen to twenty feet deep. From the look of it, I was standing at the narrowest point of the chasm. I sank down to calculate and consider. The only way to get across was for Sol to jump, and he would do that only with me on his back to force him. Ten, twelve feet at the most, I thought. I stood and turned to Sol. "Can you do it? Sure you can. We need to get to the River."

I took off the empty waterbag. Then, I stripped the saddle of the sleeping bag, saddlebags, rope, and canteen. I unbelted my gun and knife, rolled them in my jacket and tied the sleeves. One at a time, I threw them across.

I swung to the saddle and walked him forward, right to the edge. He lowered his head, looked down and blew heavily. I reined him back to start the approach.

With the touch of my spurs he jumped into a gallop. With my knees tight against the saddle I rose in the stirrups and gave him his head. With a powerful leap we flew through empty space. I had never jumped this dapple gray. When his hooves reached the lower, opposite ledge his front legs buckled and we went tumbling in a cloud of dust on the other side. As we rolled to a halt, Sol's head slammed against my side and the reins snapped from my hand. Painfully I doubled up, and with hooves scraping the ground in front of my face, I lay stunned by the impact. When I looked again Sol was up, near the chasm and blowing fearfully.

"Sol!"

The thought of losing him got me to my knees. He stood still as I crawled for the dangling reins and slipped my hand through the loop. I closed my eyes and curled up again. It was dark and then it was light and vision of the outcast Zuni woman was there in all her glory, reaching out to help me. Then she vanished.

I awoke wide-eyed and looked around, hurting with each breath. I got to my knees and probed for the source of my pain. My ribs! Are they broken? I straightened up slowly and took a slow deep breath. It was much easier. I wrapped the reins over a bush and after examining the hairless abrasions on Sol's knees, went about stiffly gathering my gear.

It was painful to ride, so I led Sol slowly for the rest of the day. At sundown, we came upon a government water tank that dictated our camp for the night. Unfortunately for me, several small bands of wild horses took turns drinking from the water tank throughout the night. Each time a wild bunch came in; they would suck up water, blow nervously and then dash away. Wanting to run with them, Sol would go berserk, raging against his rope. Afraid that he might break loose, I spent the night calming his bursts of frenzy and feeling guilty. I understood Sol's desire to be free, but it was my time to be free, and I needed him for that.

The following day was slow going. With my side hurting and my spurs clattering over rocky slabs, I led Sol through monumental cliffs and sandstone buttes. It was a region of yellow weeds, grass and prehistoric riverbeds. There was a sudden loud screeching. I thought it was a hawk. I reached for my canteen and paused to look around as I drank. Water dribbled down my chin as I searched the red cliffs and towering buttes.

High against a wall a hundred yards away, something moved. I dug in a saddlebag for my binoculars and leaned against Sol to focus. It was the Indian outcast from the trading post Tsegi, and I was not hallucinating. She raised her hands skyward and began wailing. I could not imagine how she got there, nor understand what I heard. Her choppy singing was over briefly and all was quiet again. She went down on folded legs and bowed her head. I waved high, hoping she would see, but there was no response and in that position she remained. I gathered the reins and utterly mystified, I mounted up and continued northeast and deeper into Monument Valley.

Wild horses running ahead of us on the Reservation.

 *js*

My goal to reach the San Juan River took longer and was far more difficult than I had thought it would be. The land that had looked from a distance empty and flat was filled with boulders, ravines and impassable washouts. But finally, still afoot and leading Sol, we crossed into New Mexico and camped on the east bank of the San Juan. The water, with its pungent smell of sulfur, was greatly inviting for my horse, my clothes, and me.

Though the bruise I had discovered on my left side the day before, was much darker and larger, I was no longer concerned. The excitement spawned by the snowcapped Rockies looming high in the distance renewed my spirit. Our most sinister foe, regional drought, was now behind us. Ahead, water would be everywhere.

While camping near the outskirts of Cortez, Colorado, Mr. Sol jumped a fence to be with some other horses.

The next morning when I retrieved him, I noticed a deep ragged cut across his left rear coronet, the flesh above the hoof.

"Damn, Sol. It's deep! You crazy? Now I've gotta worry about that forever. Come on, dammit!"

I could not keep a patch on it because of weeds and wet grass. I once pulled a live grasshopper from the cut, which opened and closed as Sol walked.

I used up a tube of A&D ointment and let Mr. Sol stand for a couple of days. I fixed a flat tire for a lady and along with some apples and sandwiches she gave me a bottle of hydrogen peroxide. Each time I tilted the bottle to pour, Sol would jerk his foot up and it would spill on the ground. I finally wised up. I decided if I held his right foot off the ground, he could not raise his left foot while I poured the peroxide. It worked, and as Sol blew heavily with a lip-quivering grimace, I let out a deranged giggle.

The day I left Cortez, I led Mr. Sol, spurs ringing and hooves clopping, into a service station on the edge of town. The attendant was on a roller board beneath a pickup with only his legs protruding. He was the only person around. His legs quickly disappeared and he stood up suddenly on the opposite side of the pickup. He stared, wide-eyed and fearful.

"What the hell?" he growled. "You scared the water out of me."

"Sorry! Didn't mean to do that. I was hoping I might get some grease. Like bearing grease?"

He came around the truck with a rag in his hands and looked out the door as if expecting to see a camera crew.

"You serious?"

"Yes! My horse's hooves are dry and chipping off. I've heard that packing them with grease would help. I'd like to try it."

After packing the hooves thoroughly with grease and doctoring the cut above his hoof, I led Sol to where the man was filling a bucket of water.

"What makes his hooves dry?" he said.

"Mostly his diet. He's been living off the natural forage. Up to now, there hasn't been much of that."

I washed up and mounted. And then, as I rode away, the man called out behind me.

"Tell ya one thing, it's the first time this station ever greased and watered a horse!"

Logbook: June 3, northeast of Durango.

Yesterday, when we reached Durango, it began to rain. The first rain since the ride started. It was wonderful and beneath black thunderclouds and against a strong cool wind, I found a place to camp in a back lot. The next morning it was raining so we took a break beneath a gravel bin. A woman, who lived in a trailer nearby, approached me with a large revolver pressed in the folds of her robe. It was a WW II .455 Webley's, made for the British Military with a ribbed-barrel. She held the gun with both hands, and was no doubt capable of using it. She told me that I was on private property. So, I took my poncho from over the saddle, gathered the reins and started out. "Wait a minute," she called out. "There's all kinds of crazy people, you know?" We eyed one another thoughtfully and then we laughed. With Sol back under the gravel bin, I sat at a table inside the trailer deck and enjoyed a hot cup of coffee.

I led Sol across the road to water him from a stream and to wash the grass and dirt from the cut above his hoof. Just as I was leaving, a small girl came running down a sandy road in my direction. She stopped on the bridge where I stood and looked at everything but me. Then, she began talking about an Appaloosa stallion her family had and said, to my surprise, that it had not been with any mares in a long time. She could not have been much older than seven or eight. I asked her about her family, and she replied calmly, "Oh, they put my father in jail... in Las Vegas. They say he killed a man." She was concentrating on an orange I had given her. When she could not peel it with her fingernails, she used her teeth instead. "But they're just saying that because the policemen don't like him."

"I bet you miss him, huh?"

"Yes. He always catches snakes for me. Little ones! They call me snake girl in school, all the other kids do."

"No kidding. Do you like snakes?"

She whipped her long blonde hair behind her back and nodded as she bit into the orange. The young mares were running down the fencerow with dust swirling through their legs. "My mama don't though. Me and my daddy always go looking around. We find everything. Lizards and..."

"Does your father own the ranch?"

"Yes, with my grandpa. Daddy's been fixin' it up. He was!" She grew silent.

We stood on a wooden bridge and looked around in the quiet day. The horses snapped at one another as they circled the field at a gallop. Grasshoppers leaped the width of the stream and the sun's reflection flashed in the water as it moved beneath us.

"Did your father do what they say he did?"

She finished the orange, folded the last orange peel and threw it into the water. Then, she walked over and said as she looked into Mr. Sol's eye. "No, another man did. They just say my daddy did it because they don't like him." I hung my gun over the saddle horn and mounted up slowly. "You hurt?" she asked, noticing my expression.

"Nah just bruised. Well, I hope your dad comes home soon."

"Do you have to leave now?" At last, she looked into my eyes.

"Yeah, I better." I tilted my hat against the sun and tightened the chinstrap. "Wish I could stay, but I got long way to go. I'll try to see you next summer. Okay?"

"Okay. Bye!" she said.

With her head leaning to one side, she watched me ride off. When I looked back, she straightened up from washing her hands in the stream. She smiled and continued waving as she walked backward up the sandy road. Then she turned and ran out of sight.

The next day I met Officer Thomas Griggs. He knew of the little girl and of her father's predicament, but he was unable to divulge any information, as a trial date had been set, he said.

Checking Sol's shoes.   Du Four

The Rockies

Mr. Sol and I started up Wolf Creek Pass against a sharp wind blowing snow in our faces. All I wore were Levis and two shirts under a light jacket. Because of the loss of my mule, I had shipped everything over the Rockies to Manitou Springs. The warm clothes I needed were there. Ironically, once over the Rockies, I would no longer need them, it would be summer.

I was truly miserably. Along with the cold, my hand was hurting. Four days earlier I had crossed a swiftly flowing stream and I was forced to hack through the underbrush on the opposite bank. The sharp points of the brush I had cut had torn open the skin of my knuckles. It was a small injury, but nevertheless painful. Without gloves, two socks covered my hand, like a mitten. I tried not to use my right hand but traveling with a horse is all physical.

At 10,850 feet, we reached the Continental Divide and cut southeast from Wolf Creek Pass into the Rio Grande National Forest. We were atop the divide, snow up to Sol's belly, and I could not ride him. The stirrups dragged in the drifts and I had to jump Sol through the deep snow.

We scaled our way over flat, slippery boulders, as the yellow sky lost its sun and the cold twilight enveloped the ice-laden forest. Where the snow was not as deep, I moved stiffly onto the cold saddle and nudged Sol forward. It began to sleet.

We rounded a narrow ledge, a sheer drop of some fifty feet on the right and a high wall on the left. I kept Sol hugged against the wall, as sleet pounded us. A cracking sound drew Sol's ears up. He shied suddenly toward the drop-off and stopped at the edge. I reined him back, spurring him lightly and just then a limb broke and ice crashed to the earth. Fearfully, Sol tried to turn back. I felt his right rear hoof slip over the edge; the other sank deeper and shuddered in the mud beneath the snow. I leaned forward against his neck to help him dig deeper, but it did not work. His front legs buckled beneath the weight. I was about to dismount from the rear when he lunged forward. He straightened up and planted all fours solidly on level ground. His left rear leg suffered the strain of full weight but we were saved from the fall. I led Sol for the rest of the day and all the next.

Great Sand Dunes. Ray Andis and I headed for Mosca Pass.   *js*

High and climbing higher in the aspens of the Rio Grande National Forest, Ray Andis and I trekked over animal trails of Mosca Pass toward the summit. Andis was a truck driver from Alamosa, Colorado who wanted to ride with me for a couple of days. It was refreshing to have him along. He knew the country and I was glad to have him for a guide.

The sun was nearly down and fog was closing in on us and the aspens that were marked by elk horn and bear claw. The swift gurgle of a nearby stream and mountain thunder was an integral part of the lush wilderness.

"Couple more miles we'll make camp," Ray said.

"At the top?"

"No, you'll reach the top tomorrow. I'll be heading back." The sleet grew ever stronger and silenced all conversation.

Two hours later, with a five-foot high windbreak holding firm against the southwest wind, we settled in. Dead leaves covered the floor of our camp and the branches above our windbreak served as an awning against the sleet.

Shortly a fire was ablaze and Ray's iron skillet bubbled hot with supper. To add a little more strength, I dropped a piece of aspen bark into the boiling coffee. We sat back in our shelter, warm and protected against the sleet.

Ray handed me a stiff paper plate and we both helped ourselves to the smoke-seasoned chopped steak, potatoes, fried biscuits, bacon and beans.

"You know, I was downright jealous when I read about you in the newspaper," Ray said.

"Really?"

"Absolutely. Then, when I saw you crossing the road right there in Rio Grande Valley, I knew I was going to catch up with you."

"Glad you did."

"I make pretty good, driving that truck. But, I tell ya what. If I didn't have a family and responsibilities, I'd go with you, however far." Ray leaned forward with the skillet and scraped more steak and potatoes into my plate.

"Think it'll sleet all night?"

"Yeah, probably get heavier..." Ray stopped talking and his eyes grew steadfast on something beyond me. "Jeff! Turn real slow, and look behind you." We stared in awe as small herds of elk paused fifty yards away and scented the air. Their breath was clouds of mist and steam rose from their backs. With a snort of recognition, the herd bounded off, crashing through the aspens. "Now there went some great steaks."

"You sound like my brother John," I said. "Anything on four legs represents food to him."

"That it does. And you can't beat elk steak."

We stared into the popping fire and the wind grew stronger and soon, the pools of water near our camp had frozen solid.

"Our windbreak's holding good," Ray said, examining the laced branches above and behind us.

"Sure nice here," I said. "Can you imagine how many humans have warmed their hands and stared into a fire like this?"

"Quite a few."

"For thousands of years... still doing it."

"Always will."

"Yeah, someone."

"What are you looking for, Jeff?"

"Same thing everyone's looking for, I guess."

"But... what is it?" Ray persisted.

"Heck, I don't know," I chuckled. "It's like an illusion... can't quite make it out. Maybe we're not supposed to find what we're looking for. Or maybe, we find it in bits and pieces as we go. You know, like experiences. Then, hopefully near the end... it will all come together... and then we'll see it all very clear."

"So, it's the journey that counts?"

"Gotta be. Look at all we'd miss if we weren't forced to search."

"Think you'll ever settle down?"

"Probably. I've always had a strong yen for two things, family and freedom. But the only way to have them both is one at a time.

"Can't argue with that," Ray said, as he collected the plates and cups. "Is that a .44 you've got?"

". 45."

"I got a bear last year."

"No kidding? Lot of bear around?"

"A few black bear."

"Grizzlies?"

"No, they're mostly north. Yellowstone, Glacier, Canada and Alaska."

"Thank God they've got a place to go."

With more wood on the fire and the blowing sleet growing stronger, we got into our sleeping bags. Ray flipped the butt of a cigarette into the flames and lowered his head to the saddle.

"You know," he said, "it's really too bad about Kennedy being killed."

"Yeah, my wife loved that guy." I pulled my hat over my face.

"You never know. He might have made a good president."

"What?" I raised my hat. "What do you mean?"

"You haven't heard?" Ray peered over at me. "Robert Kennedy was shot and killed last week."

I sat up. "Robert Kennedy? Killed?"

"June the fifth, I think. Some goof in Los Angeles."

"Oh, no! I thought you were talking about John Kennedy. I just shook hands with Robert... right before I left. God! First, John. Then, Martin Luther King. Now, Robert? What the hell's this country coming to?"

For some reason I took my gun from inside my sleeping bag and tossed it into the darkness. I lay there, unable to sleep. "People do stupid things." Minutes later, I was crawling around in the blowing sleet to retrieve my gun. I wiped it off and tucked it in beside me.

At sunup, we had a quiet breakfast of coffee, scrambled eggs, and yellow hominy. We saddled the horses and as the sunlight spilled warmly through the trees we took photographs of one another. I tried to give Ray the gloves I had borrowed the day before but he waved back the offer.

"You need'em more than me," he said.

Then, with a thoughtful and final examination of the campsite, we shook hands, and then went to mounted up.

"Watch out for bears." Ray said and grinned.

"You watch out too and thanks for everything."

"You'll reach the top by noon." he said as he reined his horse close and handed me two candy bars. Then Ray started back down the trail. It had been a good visit with a great guy. Feeling a little empty, I halted and I called out to him.

"I'll drop you a card from Manitou Springs." He raised his hand and that was that.

I watched until he went out of sight and then, alone again, I reined Sol toward the snow covered mountains ahead.

Ray Andis and I had shared the most precious gift of all, time!

On the western slope of the Sangre de Cristo Range.   Ray Andis

At noon, and in the midst of a great silence, we paused. The snow had let up and the wind was a whisper. I urged Sol forward and at last we stood amongst moving clouds on the Great Divide. We were at the very peak of the Sangre de Cristo Range. As I turned in awe, sunlight splashed through dark clouds etching out shadows in the snow.

In the south, mountain peaks were like islands in an ocean of clouds. The wide canyons in the north were green and the foothill's slops were trimmed in drifts of melting snow. Grey fog was lifting from blue lakes and valley streams. I drew my companion closer.

"Look, Sol. What greater glory can there be?"

I found myself wishing that time would stop. That the beauty would stay just as it was forever, with Sol and I part of it.

An hour later the sun was gone. It was growing colder and clouds were over us again. I tightened the cinch and gave Sol a pat. "Just think, Sol. John Fremont or Jim Bridger may have stood right here on this very spot." I tugged at the reins and we started down the eastern slopes. "Maybe just you and me."

I dismounted on the bed of an old narrow-gauge railroad, then stopped suddenly and reached for my gun. I drew back the hammer, moved ahead of my horse and aimed low into a thicket. The loud blast made Sol flinch a little, but he was used to it. I tied the reins to a bush and returned, holding out a blackbird.

"Supper, Sol. My last shot shell."

A mile farther we paused on the edge of a meadow with a rushing stream in the aspens nearby. I couldn't believe what I saw growing right in front of me.

"Asparagus!" I led Sol into an open area of warm sunlight, the perfect place to camp. I spread the saddle beneath a tree and began cutting wild asparagus. "You like asparagus, Sol?"

On the edge of a clear, rock-bottomed stream I took off my boots and socks and rolled up my jeans. Several trout were moving below me only a few feet away. I stepped into the water, sucked in a shivering breath and waded out. Three trout, their tails waving, drifted into a shallow pocket against a large boulder. I eased my hands into the water and went for the largest of the three. In a sudden splash, they were gone. I could not take the cold water any longer. I waded ashore, fell to the grass, and wrapped my feet in a jacket until the pain subsided. Then, I went to my saddle and returned with my .45. I used the boulder to lie on. The fish were back again. I aimed and fired. With the roar, a smoke ring rushed over the water and two fish, stunned by the impact, rolled to the surface. I stepped in and threw them to the bank.

After a supper of trout, bird breast and asparagus, I went for my sleeping bag and took Sol some asparagus on the way. He declined, so I ate it myself. Then, I got in my sleeping bag, gave thanks for a good day and went to sleep.

Logbook: June 10, I think.

Sol looks bad. I can tell he's weak by the way he moves and eats. I can even see it in his eyes. His ribs are showing. We both have lost a lot of weight. I feel tired all the time. Even when I get enough to eat, I still feel weak. It must be the same with Sol. The old town of Cripple Creek is far behind us now. Manitou Springs cannot be too much farther. I have one dime in my pocket and three .45 cartridges left. Hope it doesn't snow anymore. I'll never like snow again.

I zipped up the logbook and put it away. With my hat over my face, I thought about the girl with flaxen hair I had seen at the Grand Canyon – the one who had danced out to meet me. She had left a note for me with an Indian woman at Four Corners on a hunch that I would stop there for water. She was right. Her note said that she had read about me in the newspaper. She knew I was headed for Manitou Springs, next to Colorado Springs where she lived. There was a number and it was signed, Claudie. Amazing, how that little note lifted my spirit and helped drive me on.

Along the San Juan River & near Westcliffe, CO. *js* & The Pueblo Chieftain

"You know, Sol, we've been working our way down ever since Cripple Creek," I said, as we trotted along, our breaths blowing heavy mist. "From the looks of all that open sky, we're running out of mountains." As the evening sun moved farther west, I began

looking for a place to camp. The widely spaced patches of snow would soon stop melting and a deep freeze would set in.

I reined Sol onto a trail that led to an opening. We entered a wide sunlit field and cut straight across, through tall yellow grass. Suddenly, and without warning, the ground fell from under us. Heart thumping, I tried to rein Sol back, but when he turned, his hooves sank deeper. We were caught in a meadow-bog. Sol got up, but with no footing he fell back and on his side. I was caught beneath him. I tried to push away, but my foot was still in the stirrup and my leg was beneath Sol. As he floundered, he slammed his head against my ribs. For an instant there was darkness. All the while we sank deeper in the heavy slush. Sol rose just long enough for me to free myself. I unsnapped one end of the reins and rolled away from him. Using a whip, I popped his rump. He turned back and fought hard to obey.

"Get out, Sol. Get out!"

Blowing fearfully, he lunged, and lunged again. Then suddenly he stood up and walked from the mire, trembling in the cold air. I followed, crawling behind him. When I got to my feet, my side was hurting and my clothes were heavy with mud.

"Your head and my ribs!" I noticed the old wound on Sol's foot. Blood was streaming. "God!"

I looked west. There was not much time, only minutes of daylight left. I knew what I had to do, and it had to be quick.

I took the reins and hurried to the nearby stream. I reasoned, while palming water over the thick mud, that water would evaporate. But mud would hold moisture and cling to my clothes. I washed Sol's injury. The bleeding had stopped, frozen in the cut. I made a half-hearted attempt to clean the mud from the saddle, but like the mud in my gunbelt, it was freezing fast. I pulled at the reins and went at a trot to the nearest ravine. The shallow gully was wide with brush and an overhanging shelf loomed against the north wind. I tied the lead rope to a root curled out from the wall.

Fortunately, the saddle blanket and hair pad were still dry, held to Sol's back by the saddle. I spread the blanket over his back, tied it with the reins and gave him a gentle pat.

"I know! You'll never trust me again, right?"

I wadded up a couple of maps, covered them with leaves and sticks, struck a match and lit it. With great anticipation, I waited. Flames rose from the maps, but only briefly. The leaves and sticks were too wet to burn. There were no dead limbs to split for dry wood, so miserably cold, I dashed for my sleeping bag. I spread the poncho, tucked it in, retrieved my gun and caramel nut-bar and then pulled the cover over my head.

"COLD!" I groaned, as I pulled my crushed hat through the slit.

Wet and shivering, I wanted to sleep, yet I feared it. I listened to the wind and thought of my wife and son. My eyes watered up and then gradually, along with the wind, my shivering and fearful thoughts moved into a dark and silent void.

I woke to a stout nudge at the foot of my sleeping bag. At first, I thought of Sol, but as the probing continued, I knew there was a problem. I could hear the candy bar wrapper being pushed around. It stopped against my sleeping bag, and with a snort and a snap, I knew that it could be nothing less than a hungry bear.

It sniffed up my sleeping bag, and then tried to poke its nose through the small slit at the zipper. It pushed my hat to one side and licked my forehead. I hooked my thumb over the hammer of my .45 but there was no way to get my gun hand out of the sleeping bag. I would have to shoot right through it.

Suddenly, Sol began blowing and rearing against his rope. The intruder moved away; I heard its scuffling over the ground through wet leaves. A loud whine brought me out of the sleeping bag. It was a bear all right, and I yelled, "Sol!"

I raised my gun as the bear stood and faced me. "Get!" I shouted. It dropped down, came closer and stood again. I took aim, but then, I raised the gun and fired above its head. To my great surprise it went bounding into a ravine and up the other side. I watched and waited and then I went to calm Sol down.

The ground fog was lifting and the dripping forest sparkled in shafts of white sunlight. A band of deer in a valley clearing looked up and watched as Sol and I passed. Gray squirrels leaped from tree to tree and dashed over the ground in front of us. Black and white Magpies fluttered and fed in berry bushes. The woods were filled with the clamor of wildlife. The shouting and jeering rose to frenzy. It was an awakening, an explosion of life all around, a lingering birth of spring. The awesome beauty and the unforgiving harshness was a humbling realization. I had been treated no differently than any other animal. Indeed! Nature has no favorites.

Logbook: June 12, I think. I've lost track!
My second rest this morning. Right now the sun is straight up. I never realized how hard it was to ride down hill. Five miles back, we came upon an old cabin. It was on the opposite side of a rock-bottomed stream where Sol and I paused to drink. As I washed up a man came from the cabin with a rifle on his shoulder and a large Polaroid Land camera.

"Man you really look real," he called out. "Mind if I get a couple shots of you and the horse?"

"Well, we're pretty tired and beat up, but go ahead I guess," I said, too weak and weary to be anything but accommodating.

He took several photographs before we reached the shade of the cabin. After smearing each picture with a felt squeegee he placed them on a stack of wood in the sunlight. Someone fired a rifle in the valley below and the man gathered up the photos and said as he hurried away, "I left you a couple there!" The man never came back. So, in as much as I was out of film, and the photos were the only record of that segment of the ride, I put them in my logbook and continued to Manitou Springs.

The smeared photos taken on the eastern slopes.   📷 Unknown

Manitou Springs

We halted at a crossroad; the tire tracks on the road meant that civilization was near. I dismounted and walked closer to read a small bullet riddled sign.

"Manitou Springs, six miles. Wow! Six miles Sol! We're practically there!" Then, without warning, my legs buckled and I fell to the ground. "What the heck?" I moved forward on my hands, straightened out my legs, and gradually got to my feet. I could not believe it. I lifted one leg then the other. I was fine.

A jeep with a canvas cab slowed down to avoid a fallen branch, and then it stopped on the road to Manitou Springs. The driver leaned over and pushed open the passenger door. He looked me up and down and smiled.

"Need a lift?"

Worried that I might collapse again, I held on to the saddle horn.

"I can't leave my horse and he won't fit in your jeep," I said. "But, thanks anyway."

"You headed for Manitou?"

"Yeah."

"Been huntin'?"

"No. Just ridin'... a long way."

"I can see that. You got a place to stay in Manitou?"

"No. But I've got a number to call, just in case."

"Well, I'll head on down the hill. If you need anything, my name's Yager. Ken Yager. Call me!"

"Ken Yager? Okay! Thanks."

As I drank from my canteen the sound of the jeep faded. With a weak grip on the reins and in the growing shadows of late noon, I started down the narrow dirt road with uncertain strides.

When we entered Manitou Springs, we skirted the town's busy streets by trekking over empty lots and back roads. Dirty and ragged looking, I wanted to stay out of sight as much as possible.

I stepped into a phone booth but after standing there a moment holding the reins and staring back at Sol, I changed my mind. I headed for the adjoining park and dumped the saddle beneath the shade trees. When I led Sol to a nearby stream he was not interested, so I brought him back and sat down to rest.

After ejecting the two live rounds from my gun, I rolled up the rig, covered it with a saddle blanket and walked back to the phone booth. I dropped my last dime into the coin slot, "Please work!" I dialed the number of the local Arabian Horses Association that Ralph Goodall had given me before my ride began.

On the opposite side of Manitou Avenue was a couple of motels and behind us more than a block away was MO's Diner. On the sixth ring a man answered. I explained who I was and described my location.

"Well, I don't know," he said. In the long held silence that followed, my anxiety grew. I watched Sol go down in the grass and roll on his side. I pressed my head into the corner of the booth and closed my eyes. "Well," the man finally said. "Truth is we're having a meeting in about four hours. I'll bring up your cross country ride on an Arabian horse… see what we can do."

Sol raised his head and then let it sink to the grass. "It'll be okay Sol," I promised.

He wouldn't eat the tall grass I offered him. He gave it a sniff then went back to his own search from blade to blade. The grass looked fine to me, but something he needed was missing. He would swing his nose over the grass, stop, and bite off a few blades and continue, completely ignoring the large bundle I had gathered for him.

An hour later, while I carefully poured the last few drops of peroxide on Sol's old foot wound, headlights probing the growing mist stopped behind me. It was Ken Yager in his jeep.

"I see you made it down the hill," he said, reaching out to shake my hand. Then, his companion took my hand.

"Hi, I'm Gary," he said. "We're a couple of saddle bums ourselves. Ken said you looked like you rode a ways."

"Well, I did actually. You got horses?"

"I've got one. Ken has four." He saw the bottle of peroxide in my hand. "Back sores?"

"No, it's his foot," I said.

Ken spoke up. "Let's take a look."

It was too dark to see so Gary moved in close and thumbed his cigarette lighter. They both studied the gash above Sol's hoof.

"Heck, that ain't bad," Ken, said as we straightened up. "My horse Ranger's got one ten times worse than that. He stuck a sharp root deep in his fetlock. How long has it been like that?"

"It happened near Cortez. It was almost healed until a couple of days ago. We got in a bog…"

"Cortez? Colorado?" Gary asked with disbelief in his eyes.

"Actually, I rode from the Pacific coast, at Santa Barbara."

"California!" Ken said, "You serious?"

"I don't look that crazy, do I?"

"Hey, come on!" Gary turned away, shaking his head.

"I believe him," Ken said.

Suddenly, I felt my legs weakening. I dropped the peroxide and reached for Sol's neck.

"You okay?" Ken reached out a helping hand.

"I think I need a little rest."

"Yeah, and a few good meals. Let's get your gear. There's room at the stables for you both. Okay?"

It began to sprinkle. They stacked my gear in the jeep and put the top up. I took a rope and climbed in the rear of the Jeep to lead Sol. Ken drove, so that Sol could follow at a walk. The rain increased and it seemed to take forever, winding our way through the foothills of Pike's Peak to reach the Crystal Hills Stables.

Ken Yager moved a couple of his horses from a corral and gave all the space to my dapple gray. He offered me a room at his home but I was worried about my horse. Sol had lost nearly a hundred pounds. I was down about twenty-five pounds myself.

That first night I stayed with Sol in the wet corral and thanked God for letting us get that far. Later, Ken showed me the stable tack room where I could keep my gear and sleep for the duration of my stay.

Two days later, veterinarian Lucky Simpson came away from Mr. Sol with a cotton ball and a large syringe. His words were very comforting as he walked past Ken and me to put the syringe away.

"I have inoculated him for sleeping sickness, which is pretty widespread right now. That large dose of vitamin B will give him an appetite. He's in good shape considering all he's been through." Simpson closed his leather case and eyed the array of supplies spread out in front of the tack house. "You mailed all that in your pack saddle?"

"Yeah, it's only half of what I started with." I turned on my donated movie camera and filmed Ken smiling self-consciously as everyone watched. After that, I reached down and handed him an automatic pistol. "Need a gun?"

"What's it worth?"

"It's a Browning Hi-Power, with tangent sights."

"What does that mean?"

"The rear sight lifts up and elevates, for long range. I'll take a hundred for it and the holster."

"Sounds like a deal. But all the guys I know have rifles. How 'bout you doc?"

"I've got a gun. No use for two," Simpson said. "What I need is that pack saddle."

"Sure, it was donated by..."

"I'll give fifty bucks for the rig. And no charge for my visit."

"It's all yours," I said and then began to empty the pack bags.

Simpson thumbed through his wallet and handed me fifty dollars.

"Great. Now, if I sell the gun I'll have more money than I started out with."

"How much was that?"

"I started out with a hundred bucks and used my last dime on a phone call, when I got here."

"No wonder you lost so much weight," Simpson said as he lifted the pack saddle to his shoulder. "That tube of ointment will take care of the cut, just keep it clean, it will eventually fade. For you, with a bit of a cracked rib you're okay, but you need to eat. All that wild meat with no fat is bad. When you're in the saddle your legs are shock absorbers and that, with all the walking, you need fat for strength. I'll check back before you leave."

When Simpson and Yager had gone, I went back to my pile of supplies. While eating a dehydrated meat bar, I found the old note in my shirt pocket from Claudie. I knew it by heart. I started to throw it away, but it had been a great source of encouragement. My curiosity was still very strong. I reconsidered.

I closed the door against the damp night and turned on the lamp. I took my belted knife and gun from the deer antlers and settled in with gun oil, rag and ramrod to clean away the weeks of neglect.

After cleaning the belt, holster and sheath, I filled the row of belt loops with the .45 cartridges and cut-down .410 shotgun shells that I had shipped ahead. I drew back the hammer a couple of times to watch the precision of the cylinder locking bolt. Satisfied, I put the gun away. After loading my camera with a roll of color slides I found a can of saddle soap and went to work on the saddle.

A couple of days later, after the newspapers headlined the story of the ride, help came in trucks, bales, and bushels. That was well and good for Sol, but not for me. After having my boots half-soled and buying a new pair of Levi's, the fifty dollars from Lucky Simpson was practically gone. I had to come up with something, or go to work.

One bright afternoon, four days after my arrival, a rent horse at the stable had caught its foot in the stirrup of the saddle. While stable hands and the lady rider tried to calm the animal hopping around on one hind foot, I went for my camera.

By the time I returned, the horse had gone down and the cinch had been unbuckled. I took a few quick shots then moved in to help by slipping the stirrup down the shank and off the hoof.

The pictures turned out pretty good. Maybe they're worth a few bucks, I thought. I got to a telephone and called *The Western Horseman* magazine in Colorado Springs. A secretary listened to my brief description of the photos, and then an editor took the line.

"What kind of pictures are they?"

"You won't believe it," I told him. "I've got some really good shots of a horse with its hind foot caught in a stirrup."

"Well, it may interest you to know, we have a picture of a horse with both hind feet caught in stirrups."

"Really?"

The dollar sign dissolved. Never once had it occurred to me that I might have sold a story of my ride to the man on the telephone.

Hundreds of miles later, near some small town in Ohio, a lady ran from her house with a copy of *The Western Horseman.* In it was an article about my ride, written by Kristine, my wife. The lady had me sign it below the photograph of Sol and me. A year later the hoof-in-stirrup photos were used in an eight-part series that I did for *Horse & Rider.*

The next morning, Ken Yager drove up the driveway and turned off the engine. For a moment, he sat watching Mr. Sol eat beyond the corral fence. Then he stepped out and walked over.

"Good morning," I said.

"Mornin'! Sol's looking' better, don't you think?"

"Yep. He's okay."

"Why is that Ralph Goodall flying in from California?"

"He just wants to see Mr. Sol. Make sure we're okay."

"You sent him Doc Simpson's letter!" *

"I know, but in Burbank, Goodall's head is on the chopping block and it will be, until this is over. This ride can be good for the breed. But if something bad happens to Sol, Goodall will be blamed." I shrugged. "He did all this for me."

"Nothin's gonna happen to that horse," Ken said, with an encouraging nudge of his fist. "I'll get a few things goin' here, and then we'll get breakfast." He started to leave and then he paused, dug in his pocket and turned back. "Ken Gregory, the stable owner, bought your gun." Without counting it out, he handed over a wad of bills and went on to the office.

"Hey, Ken," I called after him, "There's a hundred and fifty here! Fifty more than I said!"

"Yeah. That's the deal," he smiled. Then, just as the door closed behind him, he opened it again and called out, "Jeff, phone!"

Ten minutes later, I hung up the telephone and stared out the large window. Ken must have seen the look on my face.

"Is everything okay?"

"Oh, things aren't going too well at home." I said as I got to my feet and moved from behind the desk.

"Anything to do with a woman?"

"Everything!" I admitted.

"Well... happens to the best of us," Ken said. "Who's the guy on the phone?"

"John Donovan."

"The guy that bet you wouldn't make it out of California?"

"That's him." I started for the door. "I'll be outside when you're ready, okay?"

"Okay. One more call, we're out of hay."

At the time, I wanted to keep my personal problems to myself so, as Ken searched over the desk for a phone number, I went out and closed the door.

John Donovan had informed me that Kristine had gotten a job at a Hollywood bookstore on Fairfax Avenue. There, she had met a guy and the two of them were together a lot.

I paused on the wooden bridge that crossed the stream to the stables. The giant cottonwoods following the stream on both sides of the bridge shimmered in the light breeze. Angry and depressed, I studied Claudie's words on the yellow paper in my hand. Then, I crushed the note and let it drop. It streaked away atop the rushing water and went out of sight.

Ken's jeep halted on the bridge behind me. "Hey! Ya hungry? Come on, let's eat."

I vaulted to the seat as Ken flipped on his new eight-track cassette tape player. The 1910 Fruitgum Company sang *Yummy, Yummy, Yummy.*

* Veterinarian Lucky Simpson's letter concerning Mr. Sol page 240.

At MO's Diner, we took a corner booth. Ken's parents owned MO's and they lived in back. Without a menu Ken called out two orders for breakfast. While we waited he spoke to just about everyone there. All I wanted to do was drink water and listen.

"Hey, that's your third glass."

"I know," I said, "I'm water-logged and still thirsty."

"Save room for food," he said.

"Tell ya this, I'll never take water for granted again."

"You won't have to worry here." Ken chuckled. "We've got plenty of that stuff."

After breakfast, Ken continued talking with his hunter friends. Each one had the same opinion on where in the high country to get the biggest elk. But Ken had his own view and would not be swayed.

"By the way," he said, offering me a cigarette that I declined, "tomorrow, we're all riding over to the Garden of the Gods and you're invited. In fact, the Jaycees... well, I told them I'd bring you. Okay?"

"Fine with me." We stood up and started for the door. Just then his parents Naomi and Bob stepped forward and presented me with a small red box. I lifted the lid. It contained the *King James Version* of the *New Testament*. It was dated, *6-27-68* and signed *"Mom & Pop" Yager*.

After thanking them, Ken proudly slapped me on the back and we went out the door.

"Talk about steaks," Ken said with an exaggerated spread of his thumb and forefinger. "The Chuckwagon steaks are that thick."

"Okay. Let's go."

"We'll get an early start so we'll have plenty of daylight. It's only a couple miles from the stables."

Ken backed into the street, turned off the eight-track and glanced at me thoughtfully.

"You know, I've been thinking about your ride and the things you been saying. Heck, I might ride with you."

"Yeah? Well, why not?"

"No, I mean it," Ken said, as the tires screeched up Manitou Avenue. "Washington! That's where to go. Make them listen."

"What do you mean?"

"We are killing the wilderness and no one gives a damn. On TV, you said someday people would have to have a license to get off the highway. It'll be the only way to protect the wilderness."

"Yeah, well, that's about it. Hopefully we're smart enough not to let that happen."

"Go to D.C., make them listen."

"Maybe they don't give a damn," I said.

"They won't if you don't tell them," he countered.

"Maybe so.

Ken turned off the eight-track and flipped on the radio. Glen Campbell was singing *Gentle on My Mind*. As the jeep snaked its way through the foothills of Manitou Springs, I wondered about Aaron and Kristine. And, I thought about the note I had thrown away and the girl Claudie who had written it.

Logbook: June 17, Crystal Hills Stable, Manitou Springs.
The Colorado Springs Free Press and the *Gazette* came to the stables to do an interview. Both Mayors Eugene McCleary of Colorado Springs and Ralph E. Sumner of Manitou Springs want to meet me tomorrow. Sol and I have been invited to appear at the Broadmoor Arena on the 29th. Guess I'll do it, and then ride out the next day.

Amid the dust and commotion of the stable, I stood back and watched Ralph Goodall examine Sol from the tip of his nose to the end of his tail.

A large gathering of horses and riders filled the air with nervous stamping and rising dust. The trek to the Garden of the Gods and the Chuckwagon festival was underway.

"Let's go Ken," a pretty girl with short blond hair called out.

"Yeah, Ken," I told him, "You guys go ahead, I'll catch up."

"Okay. We put your saddle on Rusty. Just follow the stream to Shriver Park. Beyond the park is the Garden of the Gods. That Chuckwagon brochure has a map in it. Think you can find your way?" Ken smiled and nudged his mount into a trot. "I'll save you a steak," he called out as all the others fell in behind. In a quiet rumble, they took the trail along the stream.

Ralph Goodall stepped and bowed through the split-rail fence and straightened up.

"He looks good," he said. "A little skinny, but hard as marble."

"Yeah, I'm pretty sure he's all right," I said. "By the way, how many Arabian horses do the Rosenberg's have?"

"Oh, about thirty five, forty, maybe."

"Amazing!"

"Mr. Sol is George's personal mount. He was training him for a cutting horse."

"Huh." We both looked at Sol. He was drooping sleepy-eyed beyond the fence. "Hard to believe he belongs to someone else."

"He may give him to you."

"Boy, wouldn't that be great?"

"By the way, you should have had this all along. It's Sol's insurance number. All you need is to get to a phone." I took the card and put it away.

"Hope I never need it."

"Me, too."

The two of us walked over to Rusty, the horse Ken had saddled for me. Goodall gave the glistening hide a few admiring strokes. He inspected my saddle, the same one he had tried out at his home corral in Tarzana, California.

"Different saddle bags, aren't they?"

"Yeah. We ripped the originals on a gate post."

"Anything you need, or want me to do?"

"Can't think of anything."

"Well, this is Manitou Springs. Which way from here?"

"East! There's gotta be a reason for this Ralph. Or, I'm just plain crazy."

"Don't worry. Believe me, you're doing exactly what we all want to do." He reached out and gripped my shoulder. "Jeff, you're free! How many get that?"

"Yeah, I guess." I smiled and cuffed him on the arm. "Thanks for everything Ralph. Glad you came."

"Me too. I think you've got the worst of it licked. Good luck!"

We waved at one another and he drove away. I mounted Rusty and watched as the car crossed the bridge and went out of sight.

At a bend in the stream where branches and leaves were piled against the bank, something caught my eye. I slipped from the saddle and leaned down. It was just what I thought. I straightened up with the crumpled yellow note in my hand. The paper was dry and the words, though considerably blotched, were still legible. I pressed out the wrinkles against the saddle. I was not sure why, but just having the note back lifted my spirit. I put Claudie's note back in its old, familiar shirt pocket and mounted up.

Once across Colorado Avenue, I put the sorrel into a smooth gallop. We leaped the stream in Shriver Park and continued at the same pace. Just as I reached the crest of a low rise, two kids, a boy, and a girl dashed into my path. The boy jumped out of the way but the girl fell right in front of us. Rusty leaped, and before the girl could take her hands from over her eyes, I was reaching down to help her up.

"You okay?"

"Yes, I'm okay."

"That was smart, to flatten down like that."

I pulled her up and the boy came over and began picking yellow grass from her hair.

"Where's your gun?" he said.

"What?"

"Your gun. The one in the news picture."

"Oh. It's at the stable with the rest of my stuff."

"That's not Mr. Sol," the girl said accusingly.

"How do you know?"

"Cause we had a class about you and Mr. Sol. He's a dapple-gray Arabian, right?"

"Right! A class, huh? You're not in school today?"

"No, but we're having our outdoor class," she said. "Anyway, it's Saturday!"

"Oh, yeah. So where's your class?"

"Come on, we'll show you." Giggling, the two dashed ahead, chanting in unison as they neared the crest. "Right... right... right," they pointed. "There!" We stopped walking. "Part of the class is at the benches. The others are with the teacher. See?"

Coming toward us was a young woman looking for the two. When she saw me, she stopped suddenly. I could tell she recognized me, I assumed, from of the picture in the newspaper.

"Come on you two," she called out. "The bus is here."

"We have to go," the girl said, looking up at me. I nodded. She released my hand and backed away. "Thanks for not squashing me. Bye, Jefferson."

"Yeah. You're welcome." I raked my fingers through the boy's hair as they hurried away.

"I'll tell my teacher, Claudie, we saw you," she called back with a happy smile. "She'll really be surprised."

"What?" I could not believe it. "Wait!"

They were already racing across the field.

With my binoculars, I leaned against Rusty and studied the VW-bus. It was the one I had seen at the Grand Canyon, and then I saw the teacher. The wind was up and her long blond hair lifted as she twirled slowly around and around, her arms extended straight out from her shoulders. The children were imitating her every move. Suddenly, she stopped twirling. The boy and girl that I had just met were running toward the teacher and pointing in my direction. I lowered the field glasses and took up the reins. It was Claudie. I felt a warm fluttering inside.

The sun was nearing the high summits and long shadows reached across the Garden of the Gods. I started out with the sorrel toward the Chuckwagon area and the sound of music.

There was an abrupt shouting, and I looked back to see a large white bus moving slowly along a winding dirt road. The children were shouting... JEFFERSON! They were gone and I waved at the cloud of dust.

Just as I reached for the saddle horn, something caught my eye. It was Claudie, like a mirage of gold moving in heat waves. She was coming in my direction.

I had tried to avoid any encounter with this mysterious Claudie. I had thrown away her note and it came back to me. I tried not to think of her. But now she was here, an image more beautiful than I ever imagined. Instead of mounting up, I turned Rusty back down the hill.

"What am I doing?"

Her head was down and her eyes were closed. I could not figure out what she was doing but she was wonderful to look at. I pushed my hat back and paused in front of her. Aside from the reality of the warm wind, the larks and field sparrows, it was like a dream. I wanted to say something, but I did not know what. I felt like an idiot standing there, holding onto a horse, and trying hard to act normal. Her eyes remained closed as I lifted her chin and her lips quivered.

"Sorry I took so long," I said.

I opened my arms and she pressed into me like a soft quilt. With her damp face against my neck, we stood silently swaying with the sunflowers in the warm summer air.

Dawn opened in the east with a magnificent array of purple and pastels streaming above the horizon. A hawk roving low over a wide meadow dropped suddenly through the morning shadows. There was a faint squeal and the large hawk struggled skyward with a small rabbit.

We were five miles from Manitou Springs. The colors of the sky reflected in the smooth water of a pond nearby were more distinct than the sky itself. I knelt beside a smoldering fire and filled two paper cups with coffee. I put one down, sat back and studied the perfectly sculpted face of Claudie.

A family of jays began shouting in the nearby trees. Claudie turned her head against the sunlight. I held out the coffee and she sat up with her back against the saddle, holding covers against her.

"Good morning," she said, smiling at me, her hand shading her eyes. "How long have you been up?"

"Since dawn." I leaned closer. "You've got the bluest eyes I've ever seen."

After a sip of coffee she sat the cup down and moved forward. She placed her hands on my knee and lowered her head against them.

"You had a bad dream," she said. "You kept saying *Sol*."

"Oh yeah, it was crazy. We were on railroad tracks and couldn't get off. When the train hit, it was terrible. I was okay, but Sol. Parts of Sol, mixed with... can you imagine... bear parts?"

"Awful."

"When you woke me up, my side was hurting."

"From the fall you had?"

"Yeah, I keep forgetting you read about it."

"Do you hurt now?" she asked, and placed her hand gently against my waist.

"I'm fine. What about you, Claudie?"

"Hey! You said my name."

"I've said it before."

"Not to me."

I shook my head. "You'll never know how many times I've said it, and read it."

"I believe you. Me too."

"What about all this?"

"You mean, us, right?"

"Yeah."

"Don't worry, okay? I just want to be with you as much as I can, that's all." She opened her hands and kissed my knee. Then she began getting dressed. "I know you can't stay."

I detected a crack in her voice and I wished that I could have told her otherwise as strolled out a ways. I have always wanted to stay where it was peaceful and loving. But no matter how much I wanted it to last, something inside always told me, *not for long.* And, so it was again, my self-*foe* filling prophecy. On and on. Paradise was always somewhere else.

After spearing the glassy smooth water with a long stem of grass, I started back. Claudie stood up and shyly turned away. Respecting her privacy, I did the same and scanned the skies, the white clouds above the endless, eastern flats.

"You picked the perfect place," I said. But in the back of my mind there was uneasiness. It warned me of an awful truth. Our surroundings were untouched and flourishing yet something was gnawing at it all. A calamity was coming. I knew what it was and I felt angry. "Now, the first thing we'll have to do is knock down about half of these trees." With a sweeping hand toward a hilly embankment, I went on. "Then we'll smooth out all those jagged boulders, so people will have a place to sit and look at the water while they're eating. But, the main thing is, we'll have a franchise. Can't you just see it? A giant parking lot cut right into the side of the hills. And, over there, where the cliff goes over the pond, a picturesque Burger Grill! And people can stand on the bank and feed leftover fries to the ducks."

I laughed, but it wasn't real, and I choked up. Baffled, Claudie came from behind and wrapped her arms around me.

"What is it, Jefferson?"

"That's what they're doing everywhere." I drew her close, to hide as I spoke. "It's not just that, it's everything. The good things I left. The bad things I've seen. It's all catching up. I know what I'm doing, but I don't know why. Yet I keep blundering on! Is it some kind of lesson, or what?"

Claudie urged me back. "Let's sit down. I'll get some coffee."

It took a couple minutes before I regained my composure. That emotional episode had taken me by surprise. But now, I had found someone I could talk to, someone who seemed to understand.

"All the wild horses are fenced in now. Except in Arizona, where cars hit them. In the middle of no place they fence them in, and where there's highways and cars, they run free."

"You've let it get too serious," Claudie whispered in the long held silence. "Yes, it is a lesson. But the bad things you've seen are not your fault. Isn't that the truth?"

"I guess. It was different when I started out. I just wanted to be free for a while. To see what it was like before it's all gone. Now I feel, you know, responsible."

"You can be free and responsible too."

"But I'm helpless to change anything. Bulldozers crawling up and down every hill makes you wanna scream out... stop for God's sake, let's think this over!" I wiped my hands down my stubble face. "So much destruction for a better life? Oh, I know its been going on forever. Maybe greed is what makes progress."

"No. It's love!" she said.

"Love of money?"

"No! Love of life makes people do what they do, not greed!" She pushed against me lovingly and kissed the back of my hand. "Isn't that the truth?"

"God, I hope so."

"You're only one person. And no one can change the world overnight. Not even a Wind Drinker."

"I guess."

"You're a messenger on a mission, what else can it be Jefferson? Tell it as you see it. That's being responsible. They'll print anything you say and people will listen."

The shadows on the edge of the meadow had grown short and the chattering jays had retreated deeper into the woods.

"You can call me Jeff."

"I like Jefferson. It's special."

"After my grandfather, Jefferson Lorenzo."

"Then, even more special."

"Okay. You know, you're pretty smart... I mean, wise. I'm glad you're here... I mean I'm glad we're together." She laid her head against my shoulder and we gazed over the pond.

"Isn't it beautiful, the clouds in the water?"

"Yeah. And it will never again be the same. There will be others, but never the same. Kinda sad, huh?"

"Yes, for those unaware of it," she said, pressing her face against me. "Each day is one of a kind. Just like us." She grew quiet.

"A messenger?" I asked.

"It's very honorable."

"I want you to have this." I showed her a silver chain. "Each link is welded. It's stronger than it looks." I put it over her head, it settled a little dull against her white blouse. "A friend, Jimmy Nighthawk gave it to me. He would like for you to have it."

"I'll cherish it forever." She kissed my chin. "It will always remind me of now."

"Now is a good time!"

"Yes," she agreed. "It's like a dream. Birds singing, everything is exaggerated. Look at all the colors, all the shades of green."

"Yeah," I said, watching her eyes shift in wonderment. "And what's great, it's not a dream, it's real." She squinted into my eyes and then looked back at the pond.

"Maybe," she said, smiling mysteriously. "But maybe not, Jefferson." She fluttered her eyelashes and got to her feet.

Then I thought of something. "Hey, I need to check on Sol."

"Just say the word. Oh, yes," she blushed in her hesitation. "My roommate Cecelia? She'll be in Denver for the week."

"Yeah?" Then I got her meaning. "Oh. Great!"

"I like it here too," she said with a grin. "But we don't have to stay here every night."

"Then let's not stay here tonight," I suggested.

"Okay. Put your stuff in the bug. I'll get the rest. After we check Sol, I'll take you there." As she turned away, I stopped her.

"I'm crazy, right?"

"Yeah, we both are."

Claudie! I will remember her always, slender and tan, blue eyes and flaxen hair, cut-off jeans and multicolored buttons crowning the toe straps of her sandals. After we met in the Garden of the Gods, we were together much of the time. She came to the stable to check on me. She showed me all her favorite places in the mountains. Then, when she learned I was getting ready to ride out, she took my saddle and gun from the tack-room and locked them away in the trunk of her car. When I went to retrieve it all, she cried and begged me to stay. But as guilty as I felt, and as much as I wanted to, I could not. We promised to meet at MO's Diner in one year. I gave her the old note and told her to keep it until we met again. Then I left her with the birds, the mountains, and a song I wrote.

Claudie

I could never tell her the world outside is blind,

To all the things she's thinking, the beauty of her mind.

I rode into a valley, I'll never find again.

A girl was there with flaxen hair, dancing in the wind.

Claudie, the sun watches you. Claudie, I'm watching too.

Blue eyes, with love showing through, don't look at me,

I cannot stay with you.

So many things she has taught me, without speaking a word.

Dazzling thoughts that taunt me, rhymes I've never heard.

I'll miss the smile that thrills me, the silent gaze – something's wrong!

Her bringing me moonflowers and singing wordless songs.

Claudie, the wind knows your name. Claudie, your life's like a game.

Strange one, what will you do, if you can't find another,

to play the game with you?

I don't know where I'm drifting, I've yet to see my sign.

And when I ride, I will think of her, the season that was mine.

I'll miss the touch that touched me and lips I could taste with my eyes.

The sunlit hair that brushed me, in summer winds that sighed.

Claudie, the birds stay with you. Claudie, wish I could too.

Moon child, laugh, do not cry, the distance between us,

is really not goodbye.

The Great Plains

With more than half the American continent still ahead of us, Sol and I struck out into the Great Plains.

I wiped my shirtsleeve against my damp forehead and looked back at the distant mountains. I thought of Claudie. I knew she was there, somewhere.

Manitou Springs was more than sixty miles behind us, and as far as I could see, all around laid an endless sea of yellow grass.

"If we could just see the top of a windmill, it'd be great, Sol."

I awoke from a dream to what I thought was a troop of horse soldiers going by. It was not a nightmare, just an eerie vision that seemed so real it made me sit up and look around. Even then, the thumping of weapons and the squeak of leather were clearly pronounced as the columns rumbled north. "General Custer and his boys," I mused. "Headed for the Little Bighorn... to get their comeuppance for what they did at the Washita."

But it was really just thunder... thunder mixed with the snarling and yelping of a pack of coyotes. It was impossible to sleep.

"Shut up!" I shouted. They went silent, but only for a moment. I reached for my gun, drew back the hammer, pointed skyward and squeezed the trigger. The harsh boom faded into an enormous hush. I laid back. "How's that for noise?" But the yelping began anew, first to the north, then all around. With my head deep in the sleeping bag and face beneath my hat, I finally dozed off.

With a nudge of his nose, Sol pushed the hat from over my face. I sat up shading my eyes to a beautiful, silent dawn. Sol's lead rope was wound so short around the saddle that he could barely move. He continued the assault, nibbling at my shoulder and blowing in my ear.

"Okay. Cool it!" I pushed his head away, stretched and unwound the rope. "So that's why you're called a nag! Where's my knife? I think I'll get me a steak off that rump of yours."

Playfully, I slipped my knife from its sheath and turned my back so that Sol could not see as I felt out an imaginary place to slice. "Right about there oughta do it. With mashed potatoes, gravy and black-eyed peas... sure gonna be tasty." To my surprise Sol turned and shoved me hard with his head. "Ah ha! So you do understand? Mr. Sol, is it? Maybe you oughta level with me. What's your real name, huh? Is it Bond, maybe? James Bond? All this time! Well, now, aren't you the secretive one?

I put the knife away and saddled up. "Yes, sir! I know a place that might be interested in a high-dollar guy like you. Ever heard of Alpo? I might give 'em a call."

I put my backpack on the saddle and as I took the lead into the sun-bleached prairie, bands of Pronghorns scattered ahead of us.

The Great Plains in the first week of July.   *js*

84

In great disappointment, the two of us stared down into the galvanized water tank. The bottom was filled with sand and tumbleweeds. We were still in eastern flats of Colorado, and surrounded by *miles and miles of nothing but miles,* as someone once said.

I dismounted and walked around the old wooden windmill. The mechanism was rusty and the wind-blades were still and punctured with bullet holes. I let my gun and backpack slip to the ground, tested the steps, and started up the ladder. When I reached the tower floor, I noticed that the pump-rod had been disconnected and the wind-blades were jammed with a stick and secured with wire. After unraveling the wire and reconnecting the pump-rod, I climbed back to the tower floor. I looked down at Sol and with the courage of my conviction I pulled the stick jamming the gears and watched in anticipation. With a loud groan the wind-blades began to turn and the pump-rod moved suddenly upward, then down with a rattling shutter.

"Hey, Sol! Water's on the way."

I stood aloft watching and waiting. Below, Sol dipped his head into the empty tank and blew an impatient breath. The blades picked up speed. The thrust of the pump-rod was ferociously but nothing happened. The resurrected artifact filled the air with a loud and dry squawking. Still hopeful, I watched the spigot protruding over the tank below but not a drop of water dripped from the blowing snout. I leaned against the derrick in defeat.

I re-jammed the wind-blades, disconnected the pump-rod, and then we started out again. Like a slap in the face, it struck me.

"We didn't prime it!" I stopped and looked at Sol, as though he had failed to remind me. "Why didn't you say something?" Then, I remembered, "That's right, you need water to prime it. We drank it all!" I tugged the reins and we continued. "Like no one ever says, ya gotta have water to make water."

Gray and black thunderheads were constantly rolling and rumbling in the north, but the promise of rain was yet to be kept. How insignificant our tiny parade was amid the vastness. A hot wind, a lack of water and grasshoppers were constant companions. Even a Wind Drinker needs water, I thought.

"Well, looky here, Sol." We pulled up short. A lone coyote paused in its tracks in front of us. The bushy-tailed critter was not in the least fearful of us. This unusual behavior was puzzling. "You blind, you got rabies or what?" The coyote drew in its tongue and turned his ears to listen. "Guess not. You one of the guys that kept me awake all night?" I remembered the jerky in my pocket and offered a stick. "Want a piece?" I pitched it to the ground in front of him. The coyote sniffed it and then snapped it up. "Compliments of MO's Diner." I took a strip for myself and gave the rest to the coyote. When I moved closer to pet the animal, it growled. "Okay." I backed off. "Good luck partner. Don't be trustin' ever guy that comes along, hear?"

We left the coyote behind and mounted the long swell of land ahead. When we finally reached the summit, where a soft breeze cooled the skin beneath my damp shirt and the sky was ablaze at sundown, we camped for the night.

The next morning I saw with pure delight, a single house and a windmill. In the corner of my eye, something was coming up behind us. It was the coyote. He walked up nonchalantly, paused and looked toward the farmhouse. It was as though he had decided to become part of our troop. Carefully, I leaned and gave him a gentle pat on the head. He looked into my face, and then dashed off down the slope ahead of us. I saddled up, mounted and headed for the beautiful windmill spinning in the distant flats.

As we approached the house along a rising dirt driveway I could hear windows banging shut and I saw shades being lowered. We halted in the yard.

"Hello in there," I called out, pointing at the windmill. "Mind if I water my horse?" There was no answer, so I nudged Sol forward. "Just water, that's all. I'll get it myself, okay?"

With canteen in hand, I dismounted and Sol rushed for the large water tank and began sucking up water. Just as I reached for the pump handle, the screen door banged shut and a stooped old woman hurried in our direction.

"I'll show you how. Ya gotta put the pin in," she said, and reached for the pump handle.

"Thanks, ma'am. I sure appreciate it."

"Well, tell me where you're goin' and where ya been?" She hung a bucket over the spigot and began to pump.

"I'm riding across the country, from California."

"Goodness gracious. What on earth struck you?"

"Oh, the truth I'd say."

"Well, it showed you the right way out, didn't it?" She handed me a dipper of water.

"Yeah, I guess." She smiled, and watched me drink all the water. I paused. "Crazy, huh?"

"You ain't crazy."

"Well, that's good to hear."

"How do you like the water?"

"Great!"

"Best in Colorado."

"Best in the world right now." I helped myself to another full dipper.

"That's a fine lookin' animal. What breed is it?"

"Arabian."

"Well, you sure ain't crazy. I came here myself in a wagon. All the way from Pontiac, Michigan to the wide-open west. It was eighteen eighty-five and I was only three. Course, wagons was all we had then, wagons, horses and oxen."

"You're eighty-seven years old?"

"Four days ago."

"Well, happy birthday. You're right, it's great water."

"God's mix," she said, as I filled the dipper and poured the water into my canteen. "Is the country goin' to the dogs?"

"I'm afraid some of it is."

"Well, you can't stop change." Her tiny brown eyes shifted in thought. "I once saw buffalo crossin' the Platte River up in Nebraska. They took all mornin' for them to cross. We called 'em stragglers. They were leftovers from the big herds they killed off."

"Still that many, huh?"

"Oh yes. Then, they were gone. Don't you know that was somethin' to see?"

"That would be something to see all right. Sorry I missed it."

"If you saw it you'd be old like me."

"That'd be all right too." I peered into the wrinkly eyes just as soft rumbling drew our attention to the gathering thunderheads in the far north.

"Thanks for the water," I said, as I hooked up my canteen. "It's pretty scarce out here. Think it'll ever rain?"

"Yes, and it will today," she assured me. "There's a couple of creeks between here and Eads. When you get into Kansas, the farms and towns get closer together."

"How far is Eads?"

"Oh, it depends on the road you take, the blacktop or the dirt. About thirty-five, forty miles."

For the first time, I noticed the coyote, lying in the shade near a shallow irrigation ditch.

"See that coyote by the garden?"

"I see the critter," she said.

"It's been following me all day. Acts like a dog."

"That's Tramp. He thinks he's a dog. He was born down in the breaks and raised right here. Been gone lately. The older he gets the longer he stays away."

"Well, I'll be. Now it all makes sense."

Just as I reached for the saddle horn to mount, the woman called out toward the house. "You kids can come out now."

To my surprise, six children came dashing from the house toward us. Two of them raced after Tramp, the others surrounded Sol and me, offering apples and oranges. Sol bit into an apple as I moved into the saddle.

"Hey, thanks a lot." As I stuffed the fruit into a saddlebag I noticed someone waving their hand behind the screen door. "Who's that?"

"That's great grandpa. He's just watching." The older girl said. "He won't come out. He's afraid of lightning." We both looked skyward.

"Where's your mom and dad?"

"Eads, they go once a week to get stuff."

Tramp dashed across the yard ahead of the two boys.

"Does he ever bite?"

"He will, if they get rough," she said. "Dad says he's outgrown us now."

"Get a dog. Dogs don't outgrow you."

"Come, children, let's say a prayer for the young man before he leaves. Dear Lord," she began in a clear voice, then paused as the children grew quiet and moved in closer. She went on amid a blowing hot breeze, a rumbling of distant thunder, and the distraction of a large array of blackbirds rising and falling over the sunbaked fields. "Thank you for sending this man on horseback." Then I remembered to take off my hat. "Though we're unaware of your plan dear Lord, we know it is good. Please keep him safe and help him find what he is looking for. Guide him Lord to the best road ahead. Amen."

I leaned and caressed the knurled brown hand. "Thanks," I said, and then told them all, "Goodbye."

I lifted my hat to the old man as I rode by. And, he was still waving when I reached the dirt road and looked back.

With a broad gaze of the land and feeling the power of nature, I found myself wishing that a herd of buffalo would appear, so Sol and I could catch up and run with them. But there was nothing, just an enormous emptiness with grasshoppers leaping all around. "It's gone," I blurted out without meaning to, making Sol's ears twitch to listen. Yes, the old days were truly gone, but I knew that God was still in the clouds.

With thunder booming overhead and dust swirling underfoot, I held a tight rein as Sol pranced nervously. Lightning streaked across the sky and sunlight flashed through dark clouds over the ground ahead of us. To my great delight, the long awaited rain began. One large drop hit the brim of my hat.

"Hear that, Sol? It's gonna rain." The old woman was right. I looked up and more drops splashed my face. Approaching from behind was a wall of rain, rolling up huge clouds of dust. It quickly caught up with us and drenched the dry earth with water. I let my head go back and the rain cooled my face.

I tightened my chinstrap and touched spurs to Sol's flanks. He jumped into a powerful run, and with the wind at our backs, we tried to catch the shadows of clouds whisking over the ground ahead of us.

I did not realize it at the time but I would look back on those moments as the peak of my mental and physical freedom. I could not imagine living any other way. Ironically, I had become a prisoner to the very freedom I sought and gained. I was obviously obsessed with the journey. Had I not been, I might have given up. Too, I had obligated myself to all the people I had met. In a strange twist, they were, at least in spirit cheering me on. They were counting on me to live the dream they would never know. So as it was, I would let nothing stop me. With eleven more states to cross, the journey ahead had become a forced march.

I sat up in my sleeping bag and scanned the horizon west. I saw something moving in the distant field. Probably a tumbleweed bouncing around in the light wind, I figured. Then, discounting it altogether, I rose to watch Sol munch on a patch of alfalfa. Far to the east, I could make out the tops of grain elevators. They stood alone just off a two-lane blacktop. The sight meant water. I was dusty and dirty and needed to wash up.

"You like wheat, Sol?"

After pulling on my boots and brushing the grass and burrs off the saddle blanket, I went to saddle up. What I thought to be tumbleweed was suddenly quite visible. It was the coyote, Tramp. He was playfully leaping from one fluttering grasshopper to another.

"Damn!" I left the saddle blanket and walked out a few yards. I went down on one knee and clapped my hands to get the coyote's attention. "Tramp! Come here!" He stopped romping and looked at me. "You can't go partner. You're not a dog." I threw a clod of dirt as close as I could without hitting him. Instead of running away he walked up, sat down, and looked in my eyes. I dropped the second clod and straightened up.

"I've got nothing to give ya. So, get! You can't go! Too many cars and people." I stomped and clapped my hands. He tucked in his tail, walked away and sat down to watch me saddle up.

There was a sudden loud crack. Someone fired a rifle and Sol jerked his head up. I heard a yelp and looked back. Tramp lay on his side. His legs were out straight and shuddering.

Sol stopped backing away. His ears were pointed toward the distant blacktop. A pickup truck was parked on the shoulder of the road. Whoever it was fired again and the bullet kicked up dirt between Sol and me.

"Hey!" I yelled outraged, waving my arms high. "You blind?"

It was so unbelievable. I ran at Sol and purposely slammed into him so hard that he, off balance, went down. I lay over his neck and held him there.

I looked for my gun but it was with my backpack and way out of reach. I heard a door bang shut. I looked toward the road. A man dressed from head to toe in black rushed from the bar ditch with a rifle and slid into the seat of a pickup. I rolled off Sol and by the time the sound of the engine had faded he was upright and blowing, the saddle hanging from his belly. He stood very still while I undid the cinch and let it fall to the ground.

"You're okay Sol," I said as I hurriedly searched him for bloody marks. I turned and looked down at Tramp's ragged body. Hurt and angry, I went to my knees. His eyes were half-closed, already dulled by dust, and his tongue lay in the grass from a gaping mouth. I wiped my hands down my face and stood up pushing them deep into my pockets. "Didn't I tell ya?"

Using my knife, I smoothed the dirt mound of Tramp's grave. I cut a sunflower stalk, notched together a cross and stuck it there.

I swung to the saddle and looked back at the mound that had not been there with the early morning sunrise. The ones Tramp trusted the most had fashioned his demise. He had been betrayed, and the horrible thought that he died thinking it was me, added the weight of guilt to my already heavy spirit. But he was home now I rationalized. And the beauty of his innocence will never change. That vision will forever be with me. I nudged Sol east.

"Bye, Tramp."

In the shade of grain elevators, I found a place to wash up. The water hose behind the scale house gave me an opportunity to wash

Sol from stem to stern. I turned him loose in a lot of green grass and sunflowers behind the parking lot. While drying off, I sank down on the running board of an old pickup, and watched wheat trucks, in the intermittent silence, come and go.

The back door of the scale house opened and two workmen carrying thermos bottles and lunch-pails came out. They called out and waved for me to join them. I accepted their friendly offer and went to sit between them, on a long wooden bench beneath a tree.

"Lunch in the shade," one of them said.

The same man handed me a cup and proceeded to fill it with apple juice from his thermos.

"How's the horse?"

"He's fine," I said. "That water sure cheered him up."

"You like salami?" He pitched me a sandwich before I had time to reply.

"Thanks."

"You say that coyote was a pet?"

"Yeah. His name was Tramp. He'd been with us, me and my horse that is, about four days."

"Well, coyotes ain't too welcome around here."

"Yeah, I noticed that."

"You think they were shooting at you and the horse?"

"Well, it seemed like it," I said. "They killed Tramp with the first shot. Why would they keep shooting?"

"Well, I wonder why they'd wanna shoot you?"

The three of us looked at one another. I bit into the sandwich, shrugged and shook my head.

"You got me!" The two men grinned at one another.

"Well, coyote hunters ain't the most careful bunch around!"

"He's right about that," the other man said, breaking his silence. "A farmer down the road got a bullet in the window of his tractor."

"Those two guys were not careless," I said.

"Did ya get a good look at 'em?"

"Not a good look," I admitted, "but one of them was wearing black clothes and a black hat."

One man coughed in his cup and the other turned away with a muffled laugh.

"Well... a real bad guy, huh?" They both began to laugh and I stood up a little embarrassed and finished off the sandwich.

"Sorry, we don't mean to laugh. But it's not every day we see a guy like you with this kind of a story and all."

"Yeah, I guess." I retrieved my cup of apple juice and sank back down between them. "I swear it's true. The guy was dressed in black and he had a silver hat band." Both men threw their heads back and slapped their hands with a final round of laughter.

"A real Black Bart," one said, wiping his eyes. "To the joy of laughter." We clanked our cups together and drank them down.

"Tell ya what, you really made our day. Glad you stopped by."

"Me too," I said. "Thanks for lunch. You both take care." Sol stepped out in high spirits and they both called out behind me.

"If Black Bart shows up, we'll check him out for ya."

"Yeah. And then we'll put that gun of his... Well, you know!"

I put Sol into a trot, drew my gun and fired it skyward a couple of times. I looked back and they were smiling big and shaking fists of encouragement above their heads.

Logbook: July 9, Eads, Colorado
Arrived late yesterday evening. Sheriff of Kiowa County, Eugene Kelley brought me a large cup of coffee and suggested Sol and I put up at the fairground. The day before a lady had reported to the sheriff that I had asked her children for a drink of water. She said I had thanked them and rode off on a horse with two guns strapped to my hips. I showed Kelley the knife that the lady thought was a second gun on my left side. This morning we stood together and had our photographs made for the news. Kelley, tall and rugged, mid-forties, and suiting the land perfectly rounded up feed for Sol and breakfast for me. I'll ride out at 3:00 p.m.

"I think your friend Goodall is wrong," Kelley said. "The worst is not behind you. It's ahead, especially the people." We shook hands and I asked as I mounted why he did not carry a gun.

"I keep one in the car, just in case," he said. "I grew up here. You know, I'd feel awkward."

I felt a little awkward too, but rode on, my gun at my side.

Coffee at sunrise in Eads, Colorado. Eugene Kelley

Grasshoppers sprayed in front of us like water cut by the bow of a boat. I dismounted in the back yard of a small farm. We had traveled six miles out of the way looking for water. The place was abandoned and overgrown with weeds. The survey map that I was using showed the farmer's name, but from the looks of the place, the boarded up doors with broken windows, the weeds growing through the cracks in the porch, the family was long gone. The windmill had been disconnected. The jammed wind blades, one missing, groaned back and forth in the breeze and the pump rod lay bent and discarded in the yellow grass. Perhaps the family had gone away for the same reason I had come, to find water.

Ahead of us, down the sandy road, a hawk leaped from a telephone pole and dove gracefully over the stubbed wheat field in search of prey. The flats of Colorado had begun to feel like the early days of the ride, a constant hot wind and no water.

Trotting along the shoulder of the road ahead of us were four Angus yearlings. They had squirmed beneath barbed wire where the embankment along the fence had washed away. The grass along the road was thick and green, far more inviting to the calves than the overgrazed pasture. One calf had torn its hide on the wire and blood glistened across its dusty rump. It occurred to me that the cows in the pasture had to get water from some place, but there was no windmill in sight. There was a large tank in the distant pasture so I figured there must be a line underground connected to a source of water not visible above ground. We paused at an open gate and inside the small empty corral stood a shed and a large water tank. There was nothing else, as far as I could see.

I dismounted and led Sol to the tank. No surprise, it was empty. A few feet away, there was a framework with a motor and a pole. An electric wire hung beside the motor and cobwebs were strung from the plug to the socket. It had not been used in a while. I tightened my grip on Sol's reins, and after brushing away the cobwebs, I aimed the plug at the corroded socket and pleaded, "Please work!"

There was an abrupt sputter followed by a sudden whir and the motor started. Sol jerked me back, and with the plug still in my hand the motor died. With a kindly cuss or two I leaned forward and tried again. This time I let go quickly and backed away. The motor sputtered then smoothed out and continued with a loud purr. We waited. Then it happened. With a belch of air, rusty water began burbling from the pipe spigot. Soon the water was clear and gushing so powerful that it pounded the opposite side of the tank. *"God's Mix,"* I said, repeating the old woman's words that had so perfectly described it. I leaned over and let the water splash my face, head, and neck. The water was cold; I filled my hat and put it on, gasping with pleasure as the water poured over my shoulders and down my shirt. Sol got all the water he wanted. By the time the tank was full, he was gobbling up grass along the corral fence.

I washed Sol's face and for all the tiny critters roasting in the sun, I threw water all over the place. Then I pulled the plug on the ancient motor.

We left the corralled oasis in a din of fluttering grasshoppers and shouting catbirds. My wet shirt was not only a cooling delight; it was also a subtle reminder as it quickly dried. Great Bend was miles ahead and as always, water determined the pace of the journey. The knowledge of its whereabouts could entice us on, change our direction, or temporarily hold us back.

Spivey and his horse Mr. Sol, in Leoti, Kansas.   📷 Leoti Standard

Logbook: July 10, Towner, Colorado.

"Two more miles, Sol, Kansas!" I told my horse after leaving Towner. Made thirty miles against a very hot wind to Selkirk, Kansas. For the most part the harvest is over. Wheat trucks grow fewer with each day. Camped in a pasture for the night, then rode on ten miles and posed for a reporter in front of the Leoti Standard. The reporter used a Polaroid and gave me two photographs where Sol and I look really goofy. From the Standard frig; I filled my canteen with cold water. And then, it was time to ride.

I was downright saddle-weary when I reached Scott City, Kansas. Bill Boyer, who worked for his father at the *News Chronicle*, solved a most important problem – a corral for Sol and oats to eat. The next day, with onlookers standing around, Mr. Sol received his fifth set of shoes. At 91 degrees, Bill Boyer, his wife Lucy and son Sean thought to bring lemonade for everyone. Then, the replacing of Sol's shoes turned into a neighborhood event. While farrier Marvin Turly put on Sol's new shoes, Boyer labeled each of the old ones with the date and on which foot they had been worn. Later, I boxed and addressed the set, *From Mr. Sol, to Mr. Goodall,* and mailed them to Ralph in Burbank, California.

At this halfway mark across America; Boyer took me to a place called Squaw's Den. In 1878, nearly a hundred years earlier, Cheyenne warriors had made a last stand there. The bluff-trimmed basin was where the women and children took refuge while the battle waged. It was the last U.S. battle with the Indians in Kansas.

Logbook: July 19, Great Bend, Kansas.
The county sheriff, who came to meet me, called the *Daily Tribune.* Chief photographer Tom Van Brimmer was out in ten minutes. I called my brother John in Oklahoma City. He said if I could wait, he and his son, John Jefferson, would come up. "Okay. When you get here, call the newspaper; they'll know where I am." Gary Thompson overtook me at the city limits. He was from the *Hutchinson News* and took photos. Tom Brimmer lined up a corral for Mr. Sol. Then, using my radio and TV voice, which takes a little more energy with all the ing's back on the appropriate words, I did a videotaped interview with Bob Dundas. My brother said that our sister Merle June called from Houston and asked about me. She wanted to go to the orphanage cemetery to find the gravesite of her childhood friend, Dorothy Hardin. Sadly, Merle June was never able find a permanent hiding place for that old memory. It just keeps coming back. Guess it will haunt her for the rest of her life.

Open range country was far behind us now, land without fences gone. And, as if the ride itself was not enough, I complied with Claudie's wish, to be *the messenger,* as I continued east. Ignorant of political implications, here is one of a few interviews.

KCKT TV – NBC NEWS

Bob Dundas conferred with a copy of the Daily Tribune. He tapped the story with his finger, and said.

"Jefferson? You say here... and I quote... A forest to lumber companies is a giant stash of money... and bureaucrats look upon rivers and lands as just another form of inventory to be exploited... unquote. Shouldn't people be up in arms?"

"Well, at least concerned!" I said.

"You say here Jefferson, and I quote... The animal world is doomed to extinction... unquote. Could you elaborate?

"Does anyone really believe that humans will stop populating the earth? Unless some unforeseen catastrophe takes us back to an insignificant number, the animal world hasn't a prayer. We could stop it, but man is never satisfied. There's just no gain in leaving things as they are. Man is a clumsy creature on the move. An explorer who thoughtlessly destroys as he searches behind every hill, tree and rock."

"Searching for what?"

"Himself, I guess. Or for meaning? Someday it will be the universe! And, the search will continue."

"Are you one of them?"

"We all are."

"And, we'll be right back." As the station went to a commercial break, Dundas wiped his yawning face. "How do you know you're right? Do you know the future?"

"No, but I know the sun will come up tomorrow... and, even if it's dark and cloudy... I'll know it's there. Man's blundering stops only when his own life is at stake."

A red light blinked and Dundas straightened up.

"We are back with Jefferson Spivey, who rode all the way from California on horseback. Jefferson, should hunting be banned?"

"No. Can't do that. We have developed the balance of our own environment, so of course, we have to maintain it. We've killed most of the predators... Now, we have to take their place."

"Do you hunt?"

"Only to eat."

"Jefferson! Thanks for riding by."

Logbook: July 23, Great Bend, Kansas.

John and little John just drove off headed for home. I'll ride out of Great Bend today. Sol is not eating like he should. He's drawn and lethargic, doesn't respond promptly to commands. They use insecticide around this part of the country. It worries me a lot. When the grass really looks bad, I cross fences at night and cut good grass for Sol. I bundle it up in my jacket and make at least three trips. Mosquitoes are carrying the sleeping sickness egg, a lot of talk about horses and cattle dying from the germ. I'm camped in an abandoned farmhouse with no back door where I sit looking out. It's on a hill and there's an old Dodge sedan parked beside an outhouse. It reminds me of the car that took my brother, and me in my mother's arms, to the orphanage when I was three. The rain just started and with that old memory it makes sad music, hitting the hood of the car.

Logbook: July 25, Lyons, Kansas.

Should have been here three days earlier. I located a vet, Charles Downing. Downing inoculated Sol against sleeping sickness and gave me a slip of paper with the names Lundstorm and Scoby. Both vets are in McPherson, Kansas. He said that Sol would need a booster in two weeks and would need a vitamin B shot to give him an appetite. I've had to use the railroad tracks to get through small towns so I stay alert watching out for trains. That train we met in the California desert made a lasting impression on Sol. Many of the rail beds that I have been on are abandoned and are the best way to travel.

Logbook: July 26, Windom, Kansas.

Morning. Well it rained all night. When I rode into Windom yesterday evening, a meadowlark fell from the sky right in front of Sol and me as we crossed a plowed field. I swung down and picked it up. There were no marks of any kind. It was a young bird and looked healthy. I put it in a furrow and covered it. Pesticides?

In Windom I led Sol to a grain elevator and a woman there offered me grain and a place to camp for the night. Before I bedded down, she let me weigh Sol. "He weighs eight hundred and fifty pounds," she called out through the window. My clothes were still wet from last night. I used the woman's quilt to dry Sol. I didn't care what anyone said, Sol looked good to me. He was solid muscle. All the feed in the world would not make him fat. I told her I would get Sol a vitamin B shot in McPherson.

"Might work," she replied. "But an appetite ain't gonna help if you can't feed him."

Truer words were never spoken. I mounted up and headed for McPherson. It was seventeen miles.

The ground along the railbed was muddy. I moved my horse to the grassy shoulder of the asphalt road. The morning wind was cold and the road was blotched with pools of rainwater. I noticed a dead opossum as I crossed the road to the other side. Something moved. I halted and looked back. Several tiny babies were scattered around the dead mother, but one of them was still alive sucking at a cold nipple. I dismounted and took the tenacious little creature from its mother's side. I looked it over carefully. It was quite cold and its eyes were closed and protruding darkly beneath sealed lids.

I placed the naked body inside my shirt to keep it warm. I mounted up and put a cupped hand over the tiny bulge. "A miracle," I whispered. It began to rain. I put on my poncho and rode on.

I dismounted in the yard of Doctor Scoby's house. My horse sampled the grass as I stretched forward, still holding the reins to ring the doorbell. It was a short wait. The door opened and a teenage girl froze behind the screen door. A hand went to her mouth to silence a gasp.

"Dad!" she called out, "there's a man here at the door." The girl was suddenly gone and I understood her concern. A rain soaked cowboy with a gun and knife, backpack and muddy boots was not something one sees everyday at their door. A short balding man took her place behind the screen. "Sorry," I said. "I hope I didn't scare anyone. Are you Doctor Scoby?"

"Yes. What is it?"

"My name is Jefferson Spivey. I'm crossing the country on horseback. A vet named Charles Downing back in Lyons gave me your name. I need to get my horse a vitamin B booster shot. And I found this."

We both looked down at the tiny animal in the palm of my hand. Scoby didn't say anything right away. I was not sure he understood, so I pushed my hand more into the glow of the porch light. "It's a baby opossum."

"That it is! We are just sitting down for supper. Take your horse over to the driveway. I'll be there in a second."

The inside door of the garage opened and Scoby came down the stairs with two teenage daughters eyeing me over his shoulders. I took the opossum from my shirt and held it out for them to see.

"I found this little guy on the road this morning. Its mother was dead, and I was just wondering if there was some way to help it?" Scoby took the opossum from my open hand, as I continued. "If I had an eyedropper and some milk, do you think it would live?"

"We'll give it a try," he said crisply, and, with the orphan in hand, he turned away and ushered his girls back into the house. "I'll have a look at your horse in a few minutes." He looked back from the doorway. "There's a chair there. Have a seat." I took off my poncho and sat down with a sigh of relief.

An hour later in the saddle and riding on, a dreadful feeling came over me. At first I was sad, and then I grew angry. Deep inside, I knew the opossum was dead. But after all the effort, I did not want to believe it. Who am I kidding? I thought. The life of that tiny creature doesn't mean a damn thing to anybody but me.

I dismounted in a thick patch of sand plums. As Sol snapped up wild seedheads I gathered plums and filled my shirt pockets. I still had three ears of corn in my saddlebag that I was savoring for evening camp. It was very hot and as usual, I was out of water. Irritated by the wet shirt beneath my backpack, I paused on the edge of an irrigation ditch and slipped out of the shoulder straps. A farm, like a shady oasis beyond the plowed field, was extremely inviting. I swung the backpack to the saddle, stretched out the reins and took the lead.

A tall man straightened up beside his tractor as I approached. He was working on the belted wheel, which powered the pump for irrigating the field. I said "Hi," but doubted that he heard me above the loud popping of the tractor. He turned off the engine and struck the wheel hub with a wrench a couple of times then faced Sol and me.

"Beautiful horse you got there. What can I do for you?"

"I'd like to get some water, if you don't mind?"

"Bring him around to the back," he said, "I'll get a bucket."

"Something wrong with your tractor?"

"No, it's the pump wheel. It's runnin' a slight bit catawampus. Darn belt keeps crawlin' off."

He invited me to stay awhile so I dumped my backpack, gun and knife at the base of a tree and then unsaddled Sol. There was a small, fenced-in lot behind the house and there I turned him loose.

"Will he catch easy without the halter?"

"Not always, but most of the time. When flies and mosquitoes are bad, I take it off when I turn him loose. He scratches behind his ears with a hind foot... just like a dog. Horses have been known to get their foot caught in a halter and they can strangle themselves trying to get out. See the sweat behind his ears? Mosquitoes gang up on places like that."

We sat down in the mowed grass. I loosened my chinstrap and let the air cool my face. Several fifty-pound sacks of grain were stacked in the bed of his pickup. Immediately, I thought of Sol.

"That wouldn't happen to be oats would it?" I grinned.

"It's seed," he said. "Be happy to give you oats if I had some. No, that's poison seed. You don't want your horse eating that."

"Poison? What do you do with it?"

"Plant it. It's been treated so the bugs won't eat it."

"You mean," I paused long enough to reach in my shirt pocket for a plum, "when you plant the seed, bugs keep away because of the poison?"

"That's right."

A warm breeze rustled the leaves overhead and tiny dust devils twirled along the road and dissolved against the wheel of his pickup. I gathered up a hand full of poison seed and examined it closely, pouring it slowly from one hand to the other. I thought of the meadowlark that had dropped from the sky in the plowed field near Windom, Kansas.

The sun was moving to the west when I saddled my horse. I shook the farmer's large, callused hand and moved into the saddle.

"Do you think birds can tell if the seed is poisoned?" The man looked up and his eyes shifted thoughtfully.

"I really don't know, hadn't occurred to me," he said.

Sol's hooves were softly thudding back on the road east by the time the tractor started up again, sputtering smoke rings skyward.

Logbook: August 6, Topeka, Kansas

Jack Bennett trailered us north from Ottawa, Kansas to Topeka. I am to open the Junior Championship Rodeo. There are several thousand people here. Campers, horse trailers and tents. Horses from all over the U.S. The rodeo event went great. Sol and I are now on our way back to Ottawa to continue the ride. Sol was so full of spunk that he knocked over a big television camera and broke the lens. Gave the cameraman Sol's insurance number, although it wasn't Sol's fault. The cameraman wasn't supposed to be that close to the arena. We were invited to appear the following evening, but I declined. I'm worried about the miles ahead and winter. Jack wanted my spurs, so he bought me a pair and I gave him mine. The new ones are solid bronze.

Logbook: August 9. East of Harrisonville, Missouri.

Sol has a habit of trying to take every farm entrance we come to. It could mean food and rest, he thinks. I feel guilty with each farm road we pass.

Yesterday it rained like the devil. Sol and I were drenched in the first downpour. Water spilled from my hat like a waterfall. Darkness came early and the wind from over the wet fields was chilly.

I found an old, dilapidated barn and draped my saddle over a long table and rolled out my sleeping bag. As I search the darkness behind the dim glow of my flashlight, my feet sloshed in my boots and I shivered in the wind wailing through the open ends of the barn.

I filled a cardboard box with ears of seed corn, shelled them one at a time in cast-iron stove lid, and then led Sol to supper at the foot of my bed. After much lifting and pulling, I managed to close the door at one end of the barn. The other end, where water sprayed inward there was no door at all. I hung my jacket and shirt on rusty nails along the wall, then sat on the table and struggled to get off my soggy boots and socks. With my trousers cuffs wet and my teeth chattering I moved into my sleeping bag. But then, water was dripping from the sagging roof. Instead of getting up and moving the heavy table, I placed my hat beneath the drip, turned on my side and lay curved around it. While rats scurried and Sol crunched and wind rattled the barn, I let out a tired breath and fell asleep.

The barn door groaned and sunlight hit the west wall. With dry socks on, I reached for my boots and a man sloshed in pools of water toward me.

"Seen you ride in last evenin'," he said in a booming voice. "If you had come across the road, you could have slept in a new barn. We use this for junk." He stroked Sol's neck while I continued pulling hard on my bootstraps. "If you want, we'll feed him some oats! And you can come to the house for breakfast. The wife's plannin' on ya comin'.

Mr. and Mrs. Hutchings were in their seventies and the regional history, some of which I knew, was more personal to them. They spoke of the burning of Lawrence, Kansas, on August 21, 1863. William C. Quantrill and his raiders had a big shootout with the Jayhawkers right on the ground where the old barn stood. It was easy to imagine the setting a hundred and five years earlier. Battle whoops and guns roaring in puffs of smoke in the hills and hollows.

"No wonder it was so noisy. Their spirits are still fighting," I said.

The Hutchings waited outside the new barn as I led Sol out. I could tell my presence spawned long ago memories for them. I took their hands, thanked them, mounted and rode away knowing I would never see them again. How final and sad my departure was.

By the time I reached Sedalia, then Otterville, Missouri, I knew what to expect as we continued east. I was being torn between my promise to Claudie, and my desire to avoid it all. Everyone knew about me. People were lined up on both sides of towns, in and out of their cars, watching and waiting.

One man sat on his porch reading the local paper. When he saw me passing he stood up.

"Are you the man I'm reading about here? Crossing the country on horseback?"

"I guess that's me," I told him.

"Well I'll be darn'," he said, as he opened the screen door. "Look here! Hadn't finished reading about him, and right there he is." A lady came onto the porch and he showed her the newspaper.

A typical welcome. California, Missouri.   California Democrat

Logbook: Evening, August 14, Munger's Station.

"You know Spivey," Mr. Munger said as he lowered his newspaper and looked at me, "half the people reading this don't give a damn if you make it to Washington D.C. And the other half, they're hoping you don't!"

"Really!" I scoffed, "Why do you think that? Are you one of them?"

"Nope! But you know how it is, nobody likes a winner!"

I headed for my sleeping bag with an incredulous laugh.

Awoke early to a red sky. Everything's wet. I hung my gear to dry, threw a towel on my shoulder and walked across Highway 50. Filled a bucket with water and washed my face. Munger, the old man I thought to be an incredible grouch had breakfast, literally on a silver platter, ready for me. Thick slabs of bacon, eggs and toast, covered with a white napkin. Coffee and orange juice too. Some things just make life worth living.

"Boy! This is wonderful," I said. Mr. Munger laced his fingers together and nodded with a straight face.

"Well, good! I want you to make it to Washington, D.C.," he said.

It's time to water Sol, saddle up, thank Mr. Munger and hit the trail to W, D C.

Logbook: August 18, Jefferson City, Missouri.
Early this morning a Mrs. Ford brought me lunch. I signed news photos for her and then she drove sixty miles back to Sedalia.
At the moment I am sitting on a bench outside Strong Building Supply, Inc. I'm getting ready to leave so want to get this down. After the newspaper got the story and the radio stations did their interviews, Jim Strong and Ruth Wilhelm, two truly exceptional people took over and made my brief stay in Jefferson City one to remember. Jim had Mr. Sol shod for the sixth time and furnished me with a cabin where we all cooked and just enjoyed one another's company. They took me to a nightclub and when the owner realized that I was the guy in the news, drinks were on the house. I even took off my spurs and danced with Ruth. Thank goodness it was a slow dance and Sol was not there to see.

It was blistering hot when I rode into Gerald, Missouri. The view, as I approached along the railbed, was backyard clotheslines and barking dogs. On the north side of the tracks that equally divided the settlement was a large sign and names of local businesses on the side of a building. First was *Citizens Bank,* probably the one who paid for the sign, Then, *Pleasant View Hatchery, Bill's Barbershop, Gerald Feed Store, Western Auto,* and twenty more.

On the south side of the tracks was a small boy shouting, *hey* and waving both hands above his head. He was in the shade of several small trees in what looked to be a tiny rest area with one picnic table. It looked good to me. I reined Sol in that direction.

When I dismounted the boy backed away shyly. He had called me over, but it was as though he could not believe what was happening. Perhaps it was his first encounter with the old truism –
Be careful what you wish for.

"Do you like horses?" I asked, unscrewing the lid of my canteen. His mouth opened shyly and he looked away nodding his head. I gulped down warm water and watched him comparing his boots with mine. "Boy, those are neat boots. Are they new?" He nodded again, and I went on. "Mine's about worn out." I lifted my foot and showed him the beginning of a hole on one of the half soles that I had put on in Manitou Springs. I hung the canteen over the saddle horn and let my backpack settle in the grass. "This shade feels good." The boy came closer as I slipped the saddle off Sol.

"Is that a real gun?" he finally asked.

"Yeah, it sure is," I said, as I turned the saddle over to dry the damp underside. "Wanna hold it?" His mouth fell open as I unloaded the gun and handed it to him, butt first.

"Golly! It's pretty." He looked at a house across the street. "My mom said you were comin' this way."

"So! You had me staked out for an ambush, huh?" I nudged him gently. "Your mom, huh? Where's your dad?"

"He's not here."

I took back the gun and flipped it. The muzzle hit on my palm and it stood there. The boy was speechless. I spun the gun into the holster and we both sat at the picnic table in the shade.

"Wish I was a cowboy."

"If you want to be, you will be."

"If I had a horse like him, I'd ride all the time."

"I'll bet someday you will."

"I mean now, if I had one I would." He hit the side of his fist on the table and looked away shyly.

"You not only staked me out, you're tryin' to get my horse! Reckon I'll have to keep an eye on you. What's your name?"

"Donny. I'm almost seven."

"You're old enough to be a cowboy."

"Was you a cowboy... when you was little?"

"No. Yeah, maybe, now that I think about it. I probably was and didn't know it. I was an orphan."

"What's that?"

"An orphan's someone who's uh, got a head start on being a cowboy. Kinda like you." He looked me straight in the eye.

"Really?"

"Yeah, really." He looked at Sol thinking it over. "A cowboy's a dreamer, a loner, and a drifter. You sure that's what you want to be?" He bounced his back against the table and nodded.

"Yep! That's what I wanna be."

"Okay. Tell ya what," I said, and took off my hat. "When I put my hat on your head, it means you're going to be a real cowboy." The hat sank down slowly to his ears and he tightened the chinstrap. "That's it! Now you're a real cowboy, ya hear? Don't let anyone tell you different. Okay?"

"Okay," he said, with a soft chuckle as he gave me back the hat.

"Now, I need to get some water for my horse."

"I'll get a bucket," he shouted. "There's a faucet over there."

Logbook: August 20, Gerald, Missouri.
Met a boy named Donny who wanted to be a cowboy, so I appointed him one. His mother brought me a sack lunch and by the time I was ready to ride, a dozen more people gathered in the tiny park. While photographer Chuck O'Brien with the *Gerald Star* snapped pictures and took notes, Donny was being a cowboy. He sat in the saddle stroking Sol's neck.

Being a cowboy is a philosophy, not a drawl, or a mode of dress. It's an inborn condition, encumbered by a nagging wanderlust in the heart and mind. That's what makes a cowboy.

Logbook: August 23, Valley Park, Missouri.
The hottest day yet, wet all over, sweat streaming down my face. The roads are crowded, many trucks rumbling by. When I reached Valley Park, was told by a woman at the stable that my horse would have to be kept at least fifty yards away. Health law, she said.

Logbook: August 25, East St. Louis, Illinois.
Was advised by the police to trailer my horse over the Eads Bridge, crossing the Mississippi River. Accepted their advice. When I got across the River I stopped at a phone booth and called the newspaper, as they had requested, but when they found out where I was they wouldn't come. The man on the phone said, "You'll be lucky to get your horse out of there." When I hung up, I learned what he meant. My holstered gun, knife, and ammunition were gone. I am now in the civilized east. One week ago, twenty-seven people died in riots.

The pressures of civilization were now unavoidable. Sectioned-off land and barbed wire fences imprisoned us to dirt roads, railroads and to the shoulders of bleak asphalt highways. No hunting, fishing, private property, keep off the grass. Insecticides and bad water made everything more difficult. There was no turning back and the only way out was east, to finish what I had started.

The East

Logbook: August 27, near Centralia, Illinois.
Halted Sol near a resort with a lake and surrounding cabins. A woman came down while Sol was hungrily eating the grass and said that I'd have to get off the premises.
"Is this your property?" I asked.
"Bought and paid for."
"Okay, I'll get."
I mounted and rode on.

The old house across the asphalt looked deserted, but there was a dog barking somewhere beyond the evergreens that surrounded the front yard. The driveway of the once stately two-story house had fresh tire marks in the deep sandy ruts and broken yellow grass between them. I nudged Sol carefully around a tilted iron gate with its rusty spears pointed outward.

A wide empty yard spread out in front of us. The place was ragged. The tall yellow grass and sunflowers stood dry and rigid in the still air. A large mongrel dog continued barking but he never came forward. He stayed pressed against the porch steps in the shade right next to a faucet with water dripping in a bucket.

"Hush!" a weak voice said as the screen door opened. With a whimper, the dog went silent and an old woman with pure white hair came down the steps and paused to look at me. I dismounted on a path of widely spaced steppingstones and tied Mr. Sol to a garden gate.

"Is that you?" she called out.

"Yeah, it's me," I said, convinced my notoriety was well ahead of me. "Mind if I water my horse?"

"My God, it is you," she said, starting down the path to meet me. "My heavens, you've come back." With open arms in her final few steps, I found myself entangled in a surprisingly strong embrace. She began sobbing quietly. Her white head pressing against me glistened with perspiration. We stood there in the heat of the day, holding on to one another.

The dog was immediately friendly, leaning against me with his tail wagging. Finally, she moved back and explored my face. "God bless you Arthur. Come. Let's get out of the sun." Clinging to my hand, she led me to the screened in porch and went up the three steps slowly ahead of me. Inside, she sat down and leaned back on the pillow of a quilted cot. On a table, I found a porcelain pitcher of water. I wet a washcloth, folded it, and placed it against her forehead. She took it and I gave her feeble hand a pat and let it rest beside her.

It was very quiet. I looked through the partly open door. No one was there.

"Are you alone here?"

"For heavens sake Arthur, where have you been?"

I swallowed dryly, pulled a chair forward and sank down.

"I... I just couldn't help it," I stammered carefully, not knowing what to say. "You know how things are sometimes."

"Yes, do I ever," she wailed softly, reaching out again. "Sister... Louise passed on, did ya hear? Lord a 'mighty I'm losing my senses. It was Laura Kay... a while back."

"Well, she's in a better place now."

"She was such a kind heart."

"Did she leave you here alone?" I persisted, trying to assess the situation. But she did not answer. I leaned back to consider and finally, she went to sleep.

Surely, there had to be someone watching after her, I thought. Knowing that I could not leave until I found out for sure, I walked back down the path and unsaddled my horse. After taking him a bucket of water, I threw a stick twice for the dog. He would not fetch, so I began exploring the property.

Behind the house, there was an old barn in disrepair filled with remnants of the past. An ancient carriage with tall narrow wheels stood with its dust covered leather seats stacked with books and photographs. One photo was of two men. One was stooped and old, the other was young and holding the reins of a saddled horse.

He was wearing a cowboy hat. In the background was the wrought iron gate, where I had entered the yard. It was upright and looked new. There was a stack of *Life* magazines. The top two were dated May 13, 1940 and August 21, 1944, ten cents each. They were filled with beautiful people, most in the prime of their lives. Cary Grant and Gail Patrick were promoting their latest film, *My Favorite Wife*. Gary Cooper and Teresa Wright were doing the same thing, with *Casanova Brown*. There was Hitler, Mussolini, and the Nazi destruction of Warsaw, Poland. Mankind's most horrendous event filled the pages. And, just like the present, because of the righteous and the greedy, and the power of both, generations of blameless young men continued the seemingly endless march to kill one another.

Hanging from the rafters were harnesses, leather collars and corroded brass bells. In a corner, covered with gunnysacks was a one-horse sled. Its leather seats were cracked and faded by time and use. On my way out, I examined an old double-barreled shotgun. The cracked butt stock had been meticulously wrapped with copper wire and the double hammers had been left in cocked positions. I let them down and stood the gun back in its rightful place. Then, I closed the door and walked back to the house.

With my hands shading my eyes I put my face to the screen and peered inside. The woman was still asleep. Satisfied that she was okay, I went to the water faucet and washed my face. After refilling Sol's water bucket I found a shady place in the corner of the yard and sat down with my back against the fence.

An hour later, a pickup with a loud muffler slowed on the road and came up the driveway to a quiet stop. I stood up as a man and woman walked toward me, each with a sack of groceries. The dog did not bark so I guessed that it was someone familiar to the place.

"Hi," the man said, "I'm Hank; this is my wife, Ellen. We saw you earlier. We have a restaurant down the road." He smiled. "We figured you might stop here."

"Yeah, always after water! The lady of the house was alone so I decided to stick around. I was hoping someone would show up."

"Glad you stopped. We're not her family, but we keep a pretty close watch on her."

"I'm glad somebody does."

"Well, we do!" his wife Ellen said, as they walked on to the house.

"If you'll wait, I'll bring you a cold pop," Hank called back from the porch.

"Yeah, okay. Thanks. I'll saddle my horse."

Twenty minutes later, I was saddled and ready to ride. Hank was leaning against the bed of his pickup with a beer in his hand. He and his wife owned a café seven miles down the road with a guesthouse behind it. I accepted their offer to stay the night.

"You can't miss it," Hank said as he took my empty RC Cola bottle. "It's the only place around and there's plenty of grass for your horse."

"Sounds good to me. I'll see you there."

The dog followed me to the dip of the driveway. He paused there and let out a soft bark as I rode on.

After a long hot shower I pulled the window curtain to one side and dried off, watching Sol graze from one patch of green grass to another. Traffic was sparse on the asphalt road that curved slowly to the northeast beyond the café. It was Saturday evening and headlights were beginning to come on. While I boiled water I searched my saddlebags for the coffee I knew I had. But then, I found the packets of instant coffee and sugar in my backpack. With coffee and logbook in hand, I sat back in a soft chair to write.

Logbook: September 4, Hank and Ellen's Café.
I should cross the Wabash River into Vincennes, Indiana sometime tomorrow. It seems I spend all my thoughtful time wishing I were back in the west. Hank said they'd be here before me, but it's late and I haven't seen them. Wish I had my gun back. Without it I can't hunt. The job I've taken on don't pay and because I need to ride each day to beat the winter, I'm pretty close to being at the mercy of someone. All I need is a poor man's gun or a rich man's gold. Ha! I found a newspaper by the kitchen sink. It says the death toll of Americans in Vietnam is 11,557. God, bless them all. I'll check Sol and go to bed.

I had just finished checking Sol's shoes and was ready to saddle up when Hank and Ellen arrived. They sat for a few minutes staring out the truck window. Then, they got out and Hank walked out a ways, he thumped his cigarette, and came toward me.

"Thanks, for letting me spend the night," I said, as we shook hands. "Great to get a shower."

"We're late because she's looking pretty bad," he said. "We took her to the hospital in Vincennes. Come on in. We're not open on Sunday, but Ellen's fixing us breakfast."

The interior of the small cafe was rustic, knotty pine, with red and white checkerboard oilcloth covering all the tables. It was quiet with an occasional automobile passing in the morning fog.

"Sleep good?" Hank said, refilling his coffee cup.

"Yeah, I did. Can I help with anything?"

"Don't know what it would be."

"Who's Arthur?"

"Arthur?" Hank studied me moment. "Beats me."

"She called me Arthur."

"Hey Ellen!" Hank called out. "Who's Arthur?"

Ellen came forward with heaping plates of scrambled eggs, fried potatoes, ham, buttered toast and honey.

"Arthur was her husband," she said.

"When I rode in the yard," I explained, "she put her arms around me and called me Arthur."

Ellen placed the food in front of us and looked at me through narrowing eyes. Then, suddenly, she sank down on Hank's lap, and buried her face against his neck. Hank pulled a napkin from its holder and pressed it against her hand.

"Arthur was drafted in the war," she finally said. "He rode away on horseback, out of that very same yard!" She looked at Hank and they stood and embraced. "He rode away and she never saw him again."

"She saw him again, honey," Hank said and winked at me. "Arthur came back yesterday."

Logbook: September 7, State Park, north of Shoals, Indiana.

Sol stepped off in a deep hole as we crossed Wabash River. Got into some barbed wire. Tore my shirt and sliced my arm. I washed it, lined up the jagged edges and wrapped it tight. Looks better today. The water here in the park is much cleaner. Can't remember my last tetanus shot. Bill Boyer, his wife Lucy and son Sean, from Scott City, Kansas caught up with me. They brought lemonade and cooked over an open fire. Once beyond Hoosier National Forest, I'll take back roads to Salem.

Logbook: September 15, Carrollton, Kentucky.

Got up from my cot in the barn and fed Sol corn, oats and timothy hay. This place reminds me of stories of old, tobacco plantations, the Ohio River and Mark Twain. The town of Carrollton has a population of around 5000. It's a place where everyone knows a stranger and watches him wherever he goes. The jail is an ancient gray blockhouse that should exist only in photographs taken during the Civil War. It has outlasted three courthouses, someone said. It looks about 30x30, with a pointed roof and surrounded by a rail fence. No matter where I look, I can't avoid seeing it. While I wash my clothes kids run up and down the isles of the Laundromat. I am now drinking coffee in the Gypsy Grill. Everyone is dressed up for church, after which they congregate here. The more I view the jail, the more depressed I become. There are people on the outside trying to see who's inside... perhaps a friend or a relative. It's right in the city square where winos sit and lay around. The courthouse is redbrick, white board trim and the steps have fallen off level. It's a grim place to behold. I'm sure that local officials consider it a good deterrent to law breakers. The judge is Robert Shelton. Everyone but the youth seems to be sneering at me. Perhaps a man on horseback is a reminder of a more difficult time than now. I'm sure glad to be a plainsman. And, yes, there are a lot of decent people here. State trooper Jerry Kieth organized a get-together with conservationists, and men from the state fish and game commission. Two small boys, brothers who befriended me came forward just as I mounted up to ride out.

"We told our mom about you and she fixed you a lunch," one said as the other stretched up and handed me a brown paper sack. With a handshake, I thanked them both. Then, Sol and I headed out. That was twelve days ago, now we're in Ohio. We just crossed the Ohio River from Maysville, Kentucky.

The road sign read twelve miles to Portsmouth but I was too tired to continue. I found a place for Sol and a man brought feed and water. Then, I laid my head on the saddle and fell asleep.

Late the following morning, I awoke suddenly. My leather whip was being dragged across my face. It was Claudie; she smiled and her blue eyes squinted into mine. Her VW was parked only a few feet away, yet I had not heard her approach. She had driven all the way from Colorado Springs to find me.

"It's really you!"

"It's me," she said. "Where's that Wind Drinker, who gets up with the dawn?"

"He's headed for Canada," I said, as she put her arms around me. It was a long and quiet embrace. Then, she straightened up and wiped her eyes.

"I thought I'd never find you," she said. "I talked to forest rangers, farmers, highway patrol, and every gas station... a whole week. I've been to Portsmouth and back, just this morning."

"Sorry. A sheriff in Kentucky brought me your letter. You didn't say you were coming."

"It was an afterthought, ha! I had some time off. Thanks again for the song. I love it dearly." She looked at Sol and hooked her thumb on the silver chain I had given her. "So, here we are again."

"Here you are. I'm not sure about me," I said. She placed her hand against my face.

"Fuzzy bear."

"My gun and knife was stolen in East St. Louis. The whole rig."

"Darn, Jefferson. I know what it meant to you."

"Lot of bad stuff going on there."

"I read about it. Come! Put your stuff in the car. Let's get breakfast. Will Sol be okay?

"Oh, yeah. A guy in that house over there. He knew I was coming. He was waiting with oats and water." With a weary breath, I went for my gear. "Everyone knows I'm coming."

"Wonderful!"

"No, not wonderful."

The cafe was just off the blacktop to Portsmouth. We sat at a table by a large window. When we finished eating, we stared out the window as the waitress refilled our cups. Claudie reached for my hand.

"What?" she said.

"Summer's over. I still have five states and the District of Columbia to cross."

"And?"

"Winter!"

"Don't worry. Guess what?"

"Tell me?"

"I rented a room."

"You did?"

"I spent the night in Portsmouth. I rented a room and I want us to go to church Sunday morning. Please?"

"Well, the Portsmouth Times wants a story and the Mayor wants to meet me. Hey, I'll call it off. I was going to anyway."

"No. Don't do that!"

"Why not? I'm sick of reporters and questions... and riding out on stage for everyone."

"But you're the messenger, remember?"

"I just want to be free. This isn't free!" I turned away, propped my head in my hands and closed my eyes.

"Don't feel bad," she said, gripping my arm. "People are reading about you everywhere. What you're doing is important."

"But all that clamor is what I rode away from."

"Jefferson, you can't go back. And you can't ride away from what's inside you."

"What does that mean?"

"I don't know," she said and then peered into my eyes. "Come on. We'll make it easy. I've got a car, I'm at your disposal. Uh, I don't mean it like it sounds. So! Do you want to check on Sol, or the room I rented?" She smiled and fluttered her eyelashes. I felt of my week-old beard.

"If I'm going to meet the Mayor, I'll need to clean up." We stood up and she leaned against me.

"I thought you'd see it my way, Jefferson."

After Mayor Odle and I had our photos made for the news, I stood with a reporter and some city officials for an interview.

Sunday morning Claudie and I went to Church. It was early mass, so we had breakfast, then went back to Mr. Sol.

There in the VW, with the doors open, we languished in silence, sunlight and shadows.

"That was nice. Thanks."

"Church?"

"Yeah. It's a new beginning."

I got out of the car and propped my boots on the bumper and put on my spurs. When I straightened up, Claudie was standing just as she had in the Garden of the Gods, hands clasped, head down and eyes shut. I raised her chin and said cheerfully.

"Wake up!" She opened her eyes, with tears bubbling.

"I feel so guilty."

"Plenty of that to go around."

"No, I mean... if not for me, you would be on your way to Canada. Isn't that the truth?"

"I made a decision. Now, I've got to see it through."

"You won't hate me?"

"You crazy?"

"We both are, remember? One more day?"

"Nah lets get it over with," I said. "In a few short months we'll meet at MO's."

"When it's over, when you're back in California you'll forget all about me."

"Ha, that's funny. Truth is I'll be looking in your eyes forever."

"Hold me Jefferson."

Logbook: September 27, Portsmouth, Ohio.
Not long after crossing a mile long bridge from Maysville, Kentucky into Ohio, Claudie caught up with me. Was interviewed by the news and met Mayor Odle. It's Sunday, the 29th, I think. Claudie and I went to church this morning. We renewed our pledge to meet at MO's Diner, one year from the day we met at the Grand Canyon. Claudie just left, headed for Colorado Springs. It's over a thousand miles, but she'll be there late tomorrow. I'll be lucky to make forty miles in the same amount of time. I'm already looking forward to seeing her again. That, along with the

memories of summer and my hard-hearted dream keeps me going. Geese are headed south and fall is in the leaves everywhere. Yesterday, Sol got his seventh set of shoes. I'll take the railbed out of here. Gotta go!

Logbook: October 2, West Virginia.
It's raining hard right now... beyond an open, ancient window. I found another tobacco barn. Spider webs everywhere. The roof leaks... it's dripping in front of me. They dry tobacco here, ha. It's all around me, hanging in brown thick rows. If I want to smoke, all I have to do is reach out and get a leaf, roll it up like a cigar, and smoke it. I tried it, pretty strong stuff. Sol is dozing in a dry corner. Wonder if he's full of memories like me? If it doesn't stop raining soon, I'll ride out anyway. If I let the weather determine what I do, I'll never get to D.C. I decided to spend the night in the tobacco barn. The rain has stopped, so I'll ride out this morning.

A gray sky and steady drizzle made the Charleston freight yard a gloomy place. The large railhead was crowded with flatcars, boxcars, flashing lights, and incoming and outward-bound trains. Dripping wet, Sol and I halted beside an open boxcar. I gave him a pat on the neck and dismounted. With the reins hooked over the door lock, I proceeded to scrape corn into my poncho. Sol was hungry, and when it was gone, I went back for a last meager handfull. "That's it." I moved closer to caress the trembling face. "Hey. I know you don't like trains, but it's the best way through." I could see the widely spaced tracks merging a hundred yards ahead. We were almost out of it. "A few more miles, there's a national forest, The Blue Ridge Mountains and Shenandoah. Now there's some history, Sol."

"Hey, cowboy!" a voice called out. I looked back in surprise as the door of the boxcar opened wider. It was a man with a thin gray beard surrounding a toothless smile. He held a bottle rapped in a paper bag in one hand and a hubcap filled with corn in the other. He leaned forward, "More for your horse."

"Thanks... appreciate it."

I took it and Sol gobbled it up from the hubcap as we walked on, through the smoke, steel and fog. I wondered about that man and wished I had stayed to talk, at least ask him his name.

Logbook: October 6. A farmer's field. West Virginia.

Spent the night here. Getting ready to ride out. Two days ago while crossing an intersection in some small burg outside Charleston a guy in an old Lincoln threw a rock, I guess at me, but the rock hit Sol instead. I know that I have to put up with all the bad stuff, but I nearly shot the guy. He should have hit me, not Sol. If another car hadn't pulled in behind the Lincoln... oh my! Thank God for self restraint. During the time I spent at the Kanawha Forest Stables, Alvada Martin who gave me my second gun said that I would be getting into some rough country. Mr. Sol has a deep gash very near his right eye. He's okay this morning. The swelling has gone down some. As I left the small town, several kids followed me down the railroad tracks. The man that owns this place said a national forest is just beyond his property. It'll be good to get there.

Following a noisy night of trains and traffic, I led Sol through a cattleman's gate and hooked the latch. The two-lane highway was only a few feet away and weekend traffic was heavy. After making sure that everything was strapped down and secured, I examined the dark cut below Sol's eye. It was still a little swollen, but scabbed over and dry. "Looks better to me Sol," I told him.

I took up the reins and moved closer to the highway. Two cars hurtled by; the driver in the rear let out a yell and waved. More cars were coming, this time from both directions. I elbowed Sol back a little, as they whizzed by. Finally, the coast was clear. Then, just as I started to cross, something caught my eye and I stopped. Four caterpillars had marched in single file onto the highway ahead of me.

"Hey! Wait you guys!" The caterpillars continued on their merry way with me cringing behind them. At that moment I knew my outlook on life had indeed changed. "Okay, lead the way!"

Sol and I got ahead of the tiny troop and in the center of the two-lane we stopped. Amid the blare of truck and car horns the traffic came to a halt. Pretending that something was wrong, I reached down and lifted Sol's hoof. The driver of a tractor-trailer revved his engine, and the large bumper and grill bounced toward us.

"Get out of the way!" he shouted.

A car coming from the south swung suddenly off the road and paused on the shoulder behind me.

"What's the matter?" he called out.

"Oh, had a flat!"

"Funny!" he said and drove away.

As the last caterpillar reached the edge of the asphalt I released Sol's hoof and straightened up. They were safe for another day.

I mounted up and raised my hat to the rows of traffic. Mr. Sol leaped the bar ditch and we entered the national forest.

Logbook: October 9. Frost, West Virginia.

We went from West Virginia to Virginia, now we are back in West Virginia again. No straight borders in this part of the country. The Appalachians are just ahead and beyond, the Shenandoah Valley. Along the winding road I picked bunches of tiny grapes and small bitter apples. I spend all my time being hungry. My eating habits have sure changed. I'll test anything thicker than a leaf that looks edible. The sun is burning through the fog. Wish I had it all on film. I'll never be able to describe the beauty around me as it really is. It's magnificent. It's like I'm inside a gigantic cathedral, with long misty shafts of pastel colors searching the wilderness floor. The leaves of the pin oaks, chestnut oaks, and black gum are all gold and magnetic. The yellow birch, black birch, basswood, and sycamore are so yellow it hurts my eyes. The red maple and leaves of the sugar maple are blotched with green-yellow, red, and russet. Red leaves are all over the ground from dogwood, black cherry, and white ash. The American elms are illuminated yellow in the ray of sunlight. Lucky me, I'm here to see it. Squirrel season opened today. A tough ride through the mountains. Should reach Harrisonburg late tomorrow.

Old wounds healing and hundreds of miles to go.　　　🐂 Doug Kneibert

Logbook: October 12, or 13? Beyond Harrisonburg.

We just crossed a beautiful rock bottomed stream. Sol is eating the grass around my boots. It may sound crazy but Sol's been acting different lately. Everywhere I go he follows. Maybe he senses something. Can he know the end is near? He keeps nudging me with his nose. Weird! Maybe he just wants the grass under my leg? He sure looks good. All the old cuts and scratches have healed. The one near his eye is almost gone. I wonder if he knows how much I care for him. I hope he does. Too bad he doesn't know what the word love means. From now on, I'll tell him every day, just in case he does. On the map, Washington D.C. is only a week away. Two miles back someone accidentally or intentionally shot at us. One bullet slapped through the leaves above my head and another bullet tore bark off a tree as we passed. It was certainly not a squirrel gun. About three hours of sun left. Better ride some. I rode eleven miles through the forest on the wrong trail. Cut across valley and found a farm with two horses. Thought I might find some feed but didn't.

"Mind if I camp here tonight?" It was getting dark and the farmer considered. "No, it don't suit me," he said. "I gotta get up early and go dig a grave." Sol and I went on and camped atop Jack Mountain.

Mr. Sol was stabled at Ft. Myer, Virginia. He was allowed to share the company of the U.S. Army caisson horses. The kind of horses used in earlier times for pulling field guns and caisson into battle. Today these horses are used for parades and funeral processions of the military and for other government officials.

While touring the stables, CWO John C. McKinney, in charge of the Caisson Platoon, introduced me to Black Jack. The once caparisoned horse that had been fitted with an empty saddle and empty boots, only to be led during the funeral of John F. Kennedy five years earlier. It was a sad time, filled with universal headlines and national heartbreak. Black Jack still stood just as straight and proud, the perfect example of an obedient and fearless warhorse.

It was as if I had re-enlisted. I slept in the barracks and ate with the enlisted men.

Upon learning that I was at Fort Myer, Supreme Court Justice William O. Douglas informed the brass that he wanted to meet me and Mr. Sol.

"Justice Douglas is ready to meet with you, Jefferson," John McKinney said as he came into the barracks of the caisson detachment where I had spent the last two days. "You'll have a military escort from here to the Memorial Bridge. From there, the Washington mounted police will take over. They will lead you to Zero-Mile-Stone, behind the White House, where your meeting will take place. All the news media will be there, so polish that saddle." He smiled and consulted his watch. "Two hours. You know, Mr. Sol's the first civilian horse we've had here. He's going to like those tailor made shoes."

It was spit and polish. Sol was given shots by a vet and Army farrier SP 4, D. Schultz forged his eighth and last set of shoes.

CWO John C. McKinney and Blackjack. The horse that carried the boots of the fallen President John F. Kennedy.　　　📷 G. Du Four/ U. S. Army

Supreme Court Justice William O. Douglas was there to meet us. Reni

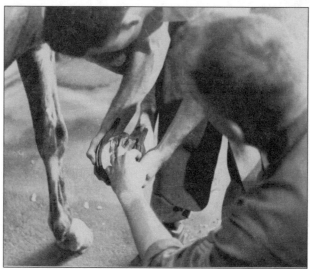

The eighth and last set of shoes for Sol. 📷 G. Du Four/ U. S. Army

"I wish I could have gone with you," Justice Douglas said as he reached up and took my hand.

I dismounted and did the only thing I could think to do for the man I so admired. I took off my hat and put it on his head.

"Now you're a cowboy," I said.

"Thank you. It's an honor," he said, tightening chinstrap.

Early Monday morning a driver, Joe Lordd, along with military photographer George Du Four, picked me up. In his office, Justice Douglas and I were unable to sit still for very long. The more we spoke of the vanishing wilderness the faster we paced. We would have been more comfortable sitting on the bank of some remote mountain stream. Before I left, he made a phone call to the Secretary of the Interior, Stewart Udall and told him that he needed to meet with me. In less than an hour, Udall and I were together, talking about trails and getting our picture made. The Trail System Act had just been approved.

Interior Secretary, Stewart Udall. October 29, 1968. 🐟 U. S. Interior Dept.

Washington International Horse Show.   📷 George Axt

Sol and I were invited to appear at the Washington International Horse Show. I accepted the invitation and we showed for a full week to honor my horse and the journey that only I knew was yet unfinished. It was still one hundred and fifty miles to the Atlantic. I received a check dated 10-30-68 from National Geographic Society for the story of my ride. It was on Riggs National Bank, so I figured it was probably good. Things were really looking up. The only thing left to worry about was the weather ahead.

Logbook: November 4, Maryland.
Very cold. I remember when my hands were tanned from the summer sun. Now they are chalk-white from the rain and cold. Just raided a turnip field. I love raw turnips. They say you are what you eat. So today, I'll be a turnip. Was stopped by police. It took my letter from Governor Spiro Agnew to get rid of them. Boy! Land of the free with a million little dictators. I dug for a turnip and rode on. Ya can't get blood from a turnip.

Logbook: November 6, Delaware.
Soaked and wet, I'll never be able to get my boots off. If I do, it'll take forever to get them back on. Very cold, hard to write. Supposed to be an Arabian horse farm a few miles beyond Georgetown. Should get there tomorrow night. National Geographic is sending photographer Robert Madden to take pictures at Rehoboth Beach. The Mayor will be there and school will let out early so all the kids can be there when I walk my horse into the surf of the Atlantic. I am sad that the ride is almost over, but I am happy as well. I feel much stronger than before I left, mentally and physically. Much of the America I went looking for is still here. A lot has been rearranged and is characterized by the times. More people, towns, highways and junkyards. Someday, someone may saddle up and look for the America I saw. I hope it will still be here. The ride has always been hard. It has been great too and sad sometimes. I've been so bitter, lonely and lost... thirsty, hungry, and sick at heart. Yet! I consider myself very lucky, this journey is a gift.
It's getting colder by the minute. Winter is closing in fast. Better ride.

Robert Madden's boss had sent him out to capture the end of my ride with instructions to use black and white film. However, he shot a full roll of color and gave it to me. Interestingly, when the *National Geographic School Bulletin* was going into print, Editor Ralph Gray decided to use one of my photographs on the cover of the April 28, 1969, issue instead of their own. It was a color shot that had been taken in the Arizona desert. The caption below the images of Sol and me read *Jefferson Spivey Discovers America.* That issue went out to eight million students. A couple of years later, two photos were made into posters. Using my camera, an unknown spectator had taken a shot of Sol and me walking along the beach. The other was one of twenty-four shots taken by Robert Madden. The color posters, bearing verses I had written, were subsequently sold all over the US. I sent one to Robert Madden and thanked him for his good work.

Quite suddenly, our race with winter was over. There was a strong chill in the air; a misty gray cloak had closed around us. School had been let out and buses loaded with children were waiting. The long ride ended on November 8.

I dismounted and led Sol down concrete steps onto the beach.

"We made it Sol," I said as a cold wave rushed up to meet us. Sol backed up, fearful of the biggest pond he had ever confronted.

Rehoboth Beach, Delaware. R. Madden/ National Geographic

As I led Sol to his homeward bound trailer it began to snow. Who would have known that of the forty-nine thousand Arabian horses in the country at the time, this particular one would be the first to accomplish such a splendid odyssey?

When we got him home I led him into the pasture and told him goodbye. All I had left was my saddle and backpack. I wondered as I watched him graze if sometime in the future when he hears the ring of spurs approaching, would he think of me?

At Rosenberg's supper table I asked, "Why did you loan me Sol?"

"Well, I thought about it long and deliberate," George said, "about two seconds. I figured if you made it, it would be a great thing. And if you didn't, no one would know about it."

Throughout the ride, I had told everyone that *Sol* meant *Sun* in Spanish. But, in this case, Sol stood for Solomon Rosenberg, George's father. He would have been very proud of his namesake.

"Goodbye, Mr. Sol."   📷 Bob Graves

The saddle weighed heavy on my shoulder as I leaned into the wind. I was the last to board Braniff flight 338 out of Greenwood, South Carolina. It was November 19, and I was on my way back to Los Angeles. The engines revved and snow swirled over the runway. It was very cold. The flight attendant stood shivering by the open door. She smiled patiently as I got aboard. I found two empty seats in the rear, just right for my saddle and me. When the door closed, I lowered my head and stared at the saddle, at the droplets of melting snow streaking the shiny leather.

Well, it's done. I had just completed a seven month, four thousand mile horseback journey living a dream. That inner voice, which makes life a little tougher for people like me, was taunting. *It's time to go back.* With a loud snap, my seatbelt locked. The plane shuddered, I think I heard it laugh as it rose triumphantly skyward.

Dark clouds moved aside and sunlight flashed through the windows. I looked down and something caught my eye. Right there in the middle of nowhere, was a man riding a gray horse. He was headed northwest and he looked just like... Wow! *My own visible spirit?* Was Trader Jim right? *"It's sorta like there's two of you,"* he had said. *"One's ancient and one's now. Each givin' purpose to the other."*

If it's true then I know where he will be. He is the soul of my purpose. He is the *Wind Drinker* in me.

The end of the long ride

Part Two

Between Rides

Back in Hollywood, about a week after the *Los Angeles Herald-Examiner* came out with the story of my transcontinental ride, I got a call from screenwriter D.C. Fontana. She said that she had been keeping up with the eight-part series *The Long Ride* that I was doing for *Horse & Rider* magazine. She was interested in the story as a screenplay. I probably should have piled it all in her lap and let her run with it. Instead, I told her I would think about it. Shortly afterwards I received a letter from Fontana, containing a list of her screenwriting credits. The list went on and on, from *Star Trek* to *Then Came Bronson*. At the time making decisions about anything was difficult, for overshadowing everything was the break up of my marriage. Now that I was home and a willing babysitter, Kristine headed for Oregon with some of her friends. In Oregon she renewed her relationship with the guy she had met at a Hollywood bookstore where she had worked. Aaron was three; the same age I was when my mother left me.

Now it was just the two of us living at a Spanish style court at 6006 Lexington Avenue. One evening while working on a knife design that I had conceived during my ride, Aaron called out from the living room.

"Dad! It looks like you."

Low and behold it did look a lot like me. It was a distant shot of actor Michael Parks in the series, *Then Came Bronson*. Instead of a motorcycle, he was on a gray horse that resembled Mr. Sol. Even the sleeping bag was strapped down in just the same way behind the saddle seat. Huh! I wonder where they got that idea.

Robert L. Jacks, producer at Twentieth Century-Fox, had just finished the film *Undefeated.* Jacks got hold of my story and took it to George Santoro, head of the story department at Universal. Santoro loved it and we got a contract. Irving Sepkowitz, with International Famous Agency, was to be our agent. How neat, I was going to be working on my own story! I was hired as associate producer and writing consultant on what was to be a world premiere of *The Long Ride*, Production Number 81424. I quit my day job modeling at the Art Center College of Design and was to report for work at Universal Studios in one week.

But first, I had a promise to keep. With Aaron in the care of his grandmother Rosemary, and all else pending, I headed for Manitou Springs, eager to see Claudie.

One year exactly from the time Claudie and I had met at the Grand Canyon I walked into MO's Diner. It was noon and the place was full of people, fond memories and tobacco smoke. With a cheerful handshake, busy Bob Yager hurried away. Naomi, his wife gave me a stout hug and pointed out an old photocopy of Sol and me that I had signed, still tacked to the wall. She said that Ken, her son was at the stable and then, she thought of something and went looking behind the counter. Momentarily, she handed me a small envelope.

"It says MO's with your name on it," she said. "It was left on the counter last week."

Knowingly I took it and Naomi went back to work. The booth where Claudie and I used to sit was occupied. I sat at the counter and ordered coffee. With my spirit sinking, I opened the envelope. The old note was there, along with a new one. It was dated, two-weeks earlier. After a quick scan of the first line I put it back in the envelope, took my coffee and left MO's.

I parked the Land Cruiser at the Crystal Hills Stables, finished off my coffee and got out to look for Ken Yager. Except for a few sleepy horses, their tails swatting flies in the warm shade, the place looked deserted. I walked over to the old bridge and there, with water gurgling below; I opened the envelope, took out Claudie's note and began to read.

Dearest Jefferson...
*Read this with a calm heart and please don't be hurt. The moments we
shared seemed so real. How could we have known it was all a dream?
Isn't that the truth? Don't worry about me... and don't wait. A Wind
Drinker must travel on. As you said in the song – The distance between
us is really not goodbye. – Forever, Claudie.*

I read it again, and then looked downstream. I saw flaxen hair
lifting in the warm breeze of her secret mountain nook. The way
she spoke, I could hear her still. *Isn't that the truth?* She would
always say, wanting only the good things in life to be true.
Claudie's failure to be there rekindled old memories of hurt and
abandonment. I was a three-year-old orphan again, still watching
and waiting for a promise to be kept, for mom to come back! I
wanted to cry out *why?* But then, I came out of my stupor to the
clamor of jays in the branches above, and I was a grown man
again. It's only memories now, I decided. And convinced it would
never be any more than that, I wadded the notes and dropped them
in the stream. They sailed away quickly, over the spillway and out
of sight into the white spume.

At least from Claudie, there was an explanation. The months of
anticipation were over. I did not even have a picture of Claudie. I
had given her the only one, a color-slide of us together in the
Garden of the Gods. Perhaps the song I wrote was indeed an
epithet. It may forever be – *The distance between us –*

I visited Ken for a couple of days and then headed back for
Hollywood to work on *The Long Ride* at 100 Universal City Plaza.

For a couple of months, it was write and rewrite, vision and
revision, but still we hit a dry hole, as an Okie oilman might say.
Though the networks had rejected thirty or so stories, *The Long
Ride* was one of two still being considered. I had my doubts. Bob
Jacks and writer Claude Traverse were making all the story
decisions. What I made was seven hundred and fifty dollars a
week, drinking coffee and nodding my head to an already decided
story line.

Geographically, the story loosely based on my ride was being
written in reverse. Instead of the trek starting at Santa Barbara, it

was to begin in New York City. "What's wrong with the way it really happened?" I tried to get the answer. But, they wanted the story character to ride away because he was forced to, not because he wanted to. The real reason was not the story they were after.

The Long Ride got the axe in favor of a story about three guys roaming around in a camper, an outdoorsman, an attorney, and a doctor. But that, 'take on any problem concept', never made it to a shooting script either, it got the axe as well.

For a short while, I had been on a Hollywood high. But when reality wrapped its little arms around my neck, Aaron and I decided to relocate our lives, get out of *Dreamtown* for good. I went to work on getting help for a national trail investigation. It was about this time that Jack Lewis, Publisher of *Gun World* magazine asked me for a story of a knife I had invent during my ride. I needed the money, so I quickly complied and picked up the check. A month later the knife I called Sabertooth appeared on the cover of *Gun World*. It was a great surprise and it gave me a notion that I would one day, years later, act upon.

Time-Life writer, Sally O'Quinn, had been assigned by *Sports Illustrated* to do a story on my trail investigation. I would be driving a Toyota Land Cruiser on this trip and trying to follow basically the same route as the '68 ride. Like then, the journey began on the beach at Santa Barbara. This time, not only was the local news present, there was a *Time-Life* photographer as well.

It was May 3, 1971. Aaron and I went together on the first half of the trail investigation. Like a couple of nomads we camped out and Aaron was able to experience the real the world around us.

Months later, while in New York City for an appearance on *To Tell The Truth*, I took a side trip to the Time-Life building where I met Don Anderson at *Sports Illustrated*. Various photographs had been sent to Anderson's office throughout the trail investigation. He showed me a stack, each larger than the norm, formatted on stiff backing. Anderson said the story was ready to run.

Shortly after the Trails project was over, Sally O'Quinn contacted me in Oklahoma City. She said that she was about to have a major operation and that she would be out of pocket for a while. Later, after it was all over with, I learned that Sally had cancer and had not survived. The story she did for *Sports Illustrated* concerning the trails and that saddle bum she loved writing about was never published.

I went to Hollywood on a mission of unfinished business. I secured the story rights for *The Long Ride* at Universal Studios, and then did some talk radio and TV appearances before heading home. Art Linkletter, host of his own show, commented that my collar length hair was, "much too long." Like a man caught in a time warp, he was unaware or in denial of the social changes around him. I saw men in the audience with hair so long they were practically sitting on it.

With me at *The Virginia Graham Show,* was actor Chill Wills. We were waiting to go before cameras and a live audience. I had met Chill years before while working at the Continental Hotel on the Sunset Strip. Chill had read about my ride, so he did most of the talking. As always, with him, it was nostalgia – the old days, and making movies with Gene Autry. It was his way of letting me know that he had gone through some tough times too. "Boy, those were the days," he said, with a thoughtful grin and a shake of his white head. "That Gene is somethin' else. When we were makin' a picture, we had to bring our own lunch. Think he'd get it sent out? Oh, no! When it rained, or at night when we weren't shootin', you think he'd get us poor actors a place to stay? Heck no. We slept under wagons. Sets with no roofs! Anything we could get under."

"No kidding?" I said, pretending to be ignorant of Gene's frugal ways. "Did he pay pretty good?" Chill threw his head back and laughed so loud that the people conducting the show waved their hands and shooed us silent.

"Boy! That's funny," Chill said. "You know how copper wire was invented? By me and Gene fightin' over the last penny he owed me." We laughed quietly with our heads down. "Lord, Lord. That Gene! You know somethin'? Ol' Gene, he could never act, he could never sing! But there's one thing he could do better than anyone else, and that's add!" Just then, the program director waved me forward.

"Give'em hell Jeff," Chill called after me. "When you see Ina, give that lady my love."

Taken from the Author's home TV. Art Linkletter and Jefferson Spivey. *js*

Four years after my first ride Mr. Sol and I were together again, making appearances at the International Arabian Horse Show in Oklahoma City. Bob Duffner, a local land developer furnished a truck, trailer and driver and together we trailered Mr. Sol all the way from Abbeville, South Carolina. That great trail horse had turned completely white, just as most gray Arabians do when they get older. It was a standing ovation as Sol and I circled the arena in spotlights and exploding camera flashes.

The first two days, hundreds of kids lined up for autographs at the Freedom Trails information booth. Many had brought with them the complete series that I had written for *Horse & Rider* magazine. I not only signed the beginning copy of the series but also endorsed each of the seven issues that followed. Some had brought *Arabian Horse World* and the *National Geographic* story for me to sign. It was a humbling experience; the line of people lasted most of the day. It was a big show with spectacles and spectators from all over the country. Some horse owners who had come to show were better known for other things: producer Mike Nichols and entertainers Wayne Newton and John Davidson had come to show their top Arabians. *Arabian Horse World* publisher Lucille Shuler was there. That great lady brought along her famous little camera and turned us all into permanent black and white blurs for the *World*.

"Hello, Mister Famous!"
I looked up from signing posters to see the smiling face of my sister, Merle June. She had come up from Houston for two things, to see me, and to go to the orphanage cemetery.
"Why?" I asked.
"I want to find Dorothy Hardin's grave. I couldn't find it last time. Maybe we both can."
The next day, Merle June and I began our solemn search for Dorothy's grave. Weeds and leaves mixed with summer grass made the place look ragged. I thought I knew where Dorothy was buried. Most of the headstones were gone and shallow depressions in the earth were the only indications of the gravesites.
Much of the orphanage grounds, except for the front of the buildings and the playground, had been turned into a public park. Beyond the bordering trees of the cemetery, joggers trotted over grounds that used to grow corn, beans, and potatoes. I remember my brother John sneaking out of the dormitory at night to bring me a large sweet potato. I kept it under my pillow, until I had eaten it all. Then, John would bring another one, until Mr. Waling, head of the orphanage farm and dairy caught him. Waling, a large man who could not have had a more appropriate name was also the orphanage disciplinarian. John reported to him on the following day and was whipped with a cut-in-half bicycle tire on his naked back and bottom for a full minute. But John was tough, we all were, and had to be. It was the nature of our lives then. From what we were told, we were living the good life. Beyond the fence was the hellish place to be.

The darkly shaded cemetery had been left unattended. I got the feeling that the place was waiting to be forgotten, and that we were perhaps the only ones left who knew of its existence. Not much longer I thought, when there's no one left to complain, a bulldozer will show up, knock down the trees and let the light in. And then, cover it all with asphalt for a parking lot.

Cuddled in a small group of trees was a plot with a wrought iron fence. It had to be the grave of a priest or a nun. Dorothy was buried in a modest grave, I recalled.

"What a shame. It used to be beautiful here," Merle June said. "You would think they would take care of it."

"It's not the orphanage anymore," I reminded her. "It looks the same, but it's not even Catholic now." I followed her gaze to the southwest corner. "I looked there."

"I'm almost positive that's where she is."

"I'm not sure anymore," I said. "Used to be more trees. Is Father Garvey buried here?"

"Oh, no. He was a monsignor, or bishop. This was for children who came and never left, like Dorothy. Father Garvey left the orphanage long before he died."

While Merle June's strongest memory of the orphanage was the day Dorothy Hardin drowned, mine was the day my mother left me there.

It was the last days of summer. I remember brown and yellow leaves and children playing everywhere. The air was fresh from an early morning rain. Three Benedictine nuns, Sister Celine, Sister Modesta and Sister Bonaventure stood waiting outside the church for my seven-year-old brother John, my mother and me.

The driver of the old sedan stopped at the gate, got out and opened it. He drove through the entrance, got out again and closed it. Then we continued up the long driveway lined with neatly trimmed hedges of crepe myrtle. We came to a quiet stop. The driver got out and opened the back door. He offered my mother his hand and Audrian Eudora, a beautiful dark-haired woman stepped out with me in her arms. While the driver held open the door, my mom paused and looked back.

"Johnny! Come on, get out," she said. With everyone watching, my brother reluctantly got from the car. Then, Sister Celine came forward and took me from my mother.

"So this is Jefferson!"

My legs stiffened and Sister Celine relented. Fearful of these women draped in black I rushed to my mother but she pushed me back. Sister Celine offered me a large silver cross, still chained to her belt. But, it was only a brief distraction. I turned it loose, gripped my hands and stared into my mother's face.

"I'm going to get you some candy at the filling station and I'll be right back," she said.

She brushed my cheek with her fingertips and went back to the car. The driver closed the door and my mother bowed her head as they drove away. I closed my eyes, pressed my fists to my mouth and held my breath. Though she said she would come back, instinctively I knew she would not.

Sister Celine lifted me in her arms, Sister Modesta took John's hand and Sister Bonaventure led the way.

"Did you know your sister Merle June is here? Sister Modesta said to my brother. John did not respond. He watched the car recede in the distance until it went out of sight.

That night, I awoke in the dark filled with fear. Moonlight was shining though the dormitory windows. I began to cry.

"Johnny... Johnny!"

"Shut up!" said a voice in the dark.

"Johnny!" I cried louder.

"Be quiet. You're gonna get a spankin'."

Suddenly, John appeared. He knelt on the floor and reached through the wooden bars for my hands.

"Don't cry, I'm here," he said.

"Where's mom, Johnny? Where's mom?"

"Shoo... you'll wake up the babies. She'll be back."

"When, Johnny?"

"Pretty soon. Go to sleep."

"Can I sleep with you?"

"No, I'll stay here."

I moved closer to my brother and held his hand against my face.

The dormitory lights came on. It was morning and John was still there, curled up on the floor beside my bed.

A bell rang and Sister Celine in her rustling black habit came over and gave John a shake.

"Wake up. Go make your bed. When you're finished, help your brother get dressed. Go!" With a cold shiver, John obeyed. Sister Modesta came into the room and the two went about their daily ritual. Sister Celine walked down the aisle between the double-deck beds ringing a bell. Sister Modesta paused at my brother's bed and looked up at Claude Boswell. He was sitting on the bunk above rigid and hesitant to come down.

"Not again!" Sister Modesta said. "You wet the bed again? Come down!" Amid giggles Boswell slipped to the floor trying to hide his wet pajamas. "Get the sheets off and turn the mattress to dry. Now! No breakfast for you." She looked at John, "You don't wet the bed, do you?" John shook his head. "Good for you. You know where the clothes bins are. Get dressed."

It was sunrise and church bells tolled with the awakening of a new day. Pigeons scattered from the bell tower and birds rose from the playground trees in shafts of sunlight.

It was after breakfast and the children were in two long rows behind the orphanage building. We were on our way to church. Boswell, red headed with his left eye missing came down the steps and joined the line behind John. John took something wrapped in a napkin from beneath his jacket and handed it to Boswell.

"What is it?"

"A biscuit," John said. "I put some butter on it."

"Thanks."

Girls filled the pews on the left, the boys were on the right. I was three, so I sat in front with others my age. With a soft rush of mysterious sing-song words, mass began. Before me was a statue of the Blessed Virgin Mary. I could not take my eyes off her. She was holding baby Jesus in the folds of her mantle. I closed my eyes to shut out the world and then, the only sound I heard was my own voice as I whispered over and over.

"Mom!"

Looking back, I realized that had it not been so painful, the memory would not be so clear.

Most of the time, the orphanage housed two hundred and twenty children. Merle June and Dorothy Hardin were like sisters. They lived in a dormitory, on the big girls' floor, with about thirty girls from ages ten to fifteen. There were more girls on the floor below.

At the time, I was seven years old and lived on the second floor of the dormitory. My brother John was on the floor above.

Dorothy died on a hot summer day. I was at the corner of the playground, up high in a Southern Red Oak I called my June bug tree. The entrance to the orphanage was a mere forty feet from where I perched. When the school bus arrived, I had just captured three June bugs of burnished-green, feasting on a watermelon rind. The bus was loaded with big girls, who had been singing when they left and were usually singing when they returned from their Sunday outing. This time, when the bus stopped at the gate there was a great hush. It was so noticeable I paused to listen.

"Spivey!" a voice shouted. I leaned through the branches and the girl called out. "Dorothy Hardin drowned!"

I reached for a limb to hold and the June bugs flew out of my hand. For a moment I was speechless.

"Where's Merle June?"

The girls in the window leaned back so that I could see. Merle June was sitting straight, her arms folded tight. She gazed up at me, then closed her eyes and bowed her head. As the bus continued up the driveway, I drew a cluster of acorns into the sunlight and studied them on the palm of my hand. They were all different, yet individually perfect. While the tiniest aspects of life held me in awe, death was a dark distraction that I could not comprehend. I did not see my sister again until Dorothy's funeral.

Mass was far more formal than any I had seen. All the boys wore white starched shirts, dark trousers, and some wore ribbon ties. The girls wore thick stockings, dresses with hems below the knees, and blouses buttoned at the collar. With the sprinkling of holy water and while the choir sang *Ave Maria,* we all filed by the open casket to pay our last respects.

When Merle June stepped forward, she laced her rosary between Dorothy's fingers. The sobbing spread and grew louder.

I had never seen a dead person before. Sadly it was Dorothy, my sister's closest friend. She looked like a beautiful mannequin. Everything was powder white, except her golden brown hair. It had been cut shoulder-length and combed straight with bangs, the style of *Prince Valiant* in the Sunday papers.

From the church, the priests and nuns, walking in pairs, separated our long columns on the warm sandy road. I was near the front, but in the lead was a station wagon converted into a hearse. It moved slowly through the oak and blackjack trees. Walking behind it was Mr. Waling. He kept his hand firmly against the casket that protruded beyond the open tailgate.

When we reached the small cemetery, the driver turned off the engine and we were all directed according to our size around the gravesite. I spotted Merle June. She stood with her hands clinging tight, while in the distance, the church bell rang out twelve times, one peal, for each year of Dorothy's short life.

The small cemetery grew crowded. Father Garvey came forward with a smoking censer. He waved it over the open grave as the casket was lowered on ropes. I turned my attention to a familiar sound and searched through the flickering leaves. My search ended when the eulogy began. In a vacuum of silence I bowed my head and thought, how strange, I had never before heard so many doves cooing in a single place.

The next day my brother John told me that he had always really liked Dorothy, and that he intended to marry her someday when he got out of the orphanage. John meant that he loved her of course but the boys of the orphanage never uttered the word love, only girls and sissies spoke that word. And because of my inability to speak that word, I never told anyone that I loved Dorothy too.

There we were, years later, standing in the same small cemetery, talking about a rosary and looking for Dorothy Hardin's grave.

"What ever happened to Sister Celine?" I asked.

"I wish I knew," Merle June said. "She was a Benedictine nun, you know. They sent them everywhere."

"I used to listen to her music with my ear to the door," I said. "One day she caught me. But she was happy that I liked her music. Once she invited me in and played Gershwin. She always kept the door closed and the music turned down. I'm not sure, but I don't think she was supposed to be listening to music. Her favorites were Schubert and Mozart. I think. She liked them all, really."

Merle June's smile faded. She sighed softly and we started the search again. Leaves rattled in the cool wind as we began clearing weeds. I started for a place I had yet to explore.

"Here!"

I looked back. Merle June was sitting with her head down. She was holding a heavy object in her lap. I knelt beside her.

"What is it?"

She held up a large chip of concrete. "A piece of her headstone with the last four letters of her name... *R, D, I, N.*" She pressed her hands to her face and the fine lines at the edge of her eyes grew deeper. "Someone should take care of this place. I should have come up. Houston is so darn far!" I gripped her shoulder.

"Merle June, it's been this way for years. At least two different organizations have occupied this place. This little cemetery's just not high on their list."

We left the chip of headstone and started for the gate.

"I know to this day, if I hadn't gotten out of that boat I would have drowned with Dorothy. Neither of us could swim. She was such a pretty girl."

"Yes, she was."

"I gave her my rosary."

"Yeah, I remember."

"Remember how they passed those donated rosaries out in shoe boxes?"

"Yeah. You got the prettiest. Pearl beads, wasn't it?"

"Yes and a silver cross. Jesus was gold. When I went by the coffin, I gave it to her. She always wanted it. I tried to give it to her once, but she wouldn't take it." Suddenly, Merle June paused and looked back. "It's still there," she said, "Dorothy still has it."

How strange it is, I thought. No matter how grand life events are, we look back in memory at the simplest ones.

"Let's go to the grotto," I said. "We know where Dorothy is. Hey! As far as I'm concerned, this whole place belongs to her." With a sad smile Merle June reached out and took my hand. We left the cemetery and closed the gate.

The grotto, the once beautiful shrine of our childhood, was sad to behold. It was all but crumbled to the ground. The dome shaped structure with an open arched front housed a statue of the Blessed Virgin Mary. Her foot held down a large snake, which represented evil. It was wrapped around a globe of the earth where Mary stood. On the ground in front of the grotto, there was a half circular curb six inches wide and made of sharp rocks pointed straight up. It is where we used to kneel and pray while doing our penance. Once, we had a picture made there with our mother when she and Lillie, our older sister, came to visit.

Mary's face was chalk white, faded by time. Her nose and chin, her uplifted hands that had perpetually prayed with us all, were broken off. The once brightly painted, definable globe could no longer be distinguished. The only visible part of the snake was a chalky headless protrusion that blended with Mary's foot.

Though the grotto was a falling image that would never regain its splendor, it would not be forgotten by generations of children who knelt in awe of its majesty. That beautiful statue once represented the imaginary Mother of us all.

We walked down the long driveway to the playground. It was lined with descendants of the crepe myrtle hedges where we once played hide-and-go-seek. The sandbox had nearly rotted away, what was left was overgrown with weeds. The fence I used to lean against watching horses beyond the highway chase one another was just as it was then. It still had the sag where I leaned my clinging weight.

In the melancholy silence, we heard an old familiar sound and looked up. A dove was cooing there above us, nesting in the shading branches of my June bug tree.

At the grotto, Audrian Eudora, Merle June, John, and Jefferson Spivey. St. Joseph's Orphanage.

 Lillie

When all the land becomes a city
and there are no forests left to inspire the poet's eye,
When a child can no longer catch the scent of wild
flowers in the wind – To me, that will be a time to die.

Freedom Trails

Freedom Trails was to be my next journey. It was an adventure that I hoped, in spirit at least, would include all Americans. On May 3, 1971 my second journey began just as before, at Santa Barbara, California. I decided to take a proclamation with me and have it signed by various VIPs and others in favor of the Freedom Trails.

The proclamation was first signed and presented to me by Sam Yorty, then mayor of Los Angeles. Editor Mary Hazell Harris, of *Defenders of Wildlife,* issued me a grant for a story that I would later do on the trail investigation. To retrace the steps of my horseback journey, I was furnished a four-wheel drive to negotiate the rugged backcountry. The Toyota Land Cruiser enabled me to go far beyond any preconceived route, as well as make a more practical study of the trails concept. In the five months that followed, I covered twelve thousand miles.

During this second journey, I made an effort to see many of the people that I had met on my ride.

I had promised to visit the old miner Ed and his dog Thor in the foothills of the El Dorado Mountains south of Boulder City, and it was a promise I intended to keep. When I returned over a washed out road to his camp, I found the place deserted. While Aaron explored, I walked over the empty grounds in sad recollection.

The once light blue trailer was nearly white. The door was off its hinges and the windows were broken, the frames bent outward and jagged. Other than the trash-heaped mine entrance, and the trailer, I could find nothing, not a letter, a photograph, or anything of a personal nature that could testify to Ed's long history there.

An hour later, on the way to Boulder City, I met a deputy sheriff parked along the highway. He remembered Ed.

"A gang of hippies beat the old guy to death. Over a year ago," he said. "I don't know about the dog."

I gazed through the window in disbelief. The sun was going down and Boulder City was lighting up in the darkening hills.

"I should have been here with him," I told the deputy as I started the engine.

"Are you a relative?"

"No, just a friend. Thanks." I waved and drove away. Angrily, I bounced my head against the steering wheel. I wanted to yell but Aaron was asleep on his pallet behind me. I found a turnout and in the darkness, atop the nearest hill, my intended roar of outrage came out as a puny whisper, "Ed!"

Cassette Log: May 9, 1971, Boulder City, Nevada.

Bob and Ann Williams, owners of the Mohave Motel, insisted that Aaron and I spend the weekend. I had met Bob during the '68 ride. He was the man who had loaned me a pickup to take the dog Thor back to Ed's mine in the hills south of Boulder. Bob took Aaron and me for a boat ride on Lake Mead. We had a great time cruising over the lake and when it came time to dock, Aaron ran ahead of us chasing Bob's dog. Apparently, the dog turned left at the end of the walkway but Aaron didn't, and no one saw it happen. Bob was talking and I was just following along on the narrow walkway in no great hurry. About the time Bob took the left turn I noticed the dog, waiting and alone on the dock. An empty feeling rushed over me and just as I made the left turn, I spotted Aaron rising face up in the deep water. It seemed so unreal. Aaron said nothing. I said nothing. Fear choked at my throat. I grabbed the walk corner pole, leaned, and snatched the front of Aaron's jacket. With all my strength, I straightened up. Aaron was hanging in my grip like a wet blanket above my head. I jabbed him gently with my fist and he coughed up water as I lowered him to the walk. Aaron was alive. Thank God. He was with us.

Aaron dripping wet and Bob Williams at Lake Mead – Stormy Hall and Aaron in Montrose, Colorado. *js*

Aaron, just four years old, with only a rough old dad around, fell in love with Stormy Hall. Stormy worked in a curio shop at the Grand Canyon. She lived with her mother and father and a twin sister in Montrose, Colorado. She was part Iroquois, as I recall, and very appealing. In the months that followed, we met again and again and shared good times at the Grand Canyon, Telluride and Montrose. We became close and when I had to be gone, Stormy took care of Aaron. She hugged him a lot and used the word love often. Each day with Stormy was a lighthearted adventure. At the time it seemed like we were the perfect trio. Aaron had balance for his expanding disposition; I had praise for my work and bullheaded belief in the future of trails. Over time however, the space between us grew wider and wider. Finally, we lost track of one another altogether. Oddly, I do not recall us ever saying good-bye. Sometimes there is no explanation for the way things turnout. Some loose ends just never get tied. Clearly there is much more to life than social and romantic ties between a woman and a man.

John Masson was a hitchhiker. At least that is what he was doing when we met. Aaron and I had stopped for a drink of water and to fill our canteens at Desert View. It was the same place where I first saw Claudie in 1968. Masson was standing along the road as we pulled away in the Land Cruiser. Because of the way he looked, unlike any hitchhiker I had ever seen, I stopped to give him a lift. He had a beard and mustache and his hair was reasonably short. He was wearing an Army fatigue shirt with sergeant stripes and white cut-offs. What was noticeably different was his fashionable backpack and sleeping bag unit. Tied to it all were a pair of expensive trail boots and a goatskin water bag with a steerhorn spout. Before we reached the fork where Masson would go south to Flagstaff and we would continue northeast to Tsegi, I learned that he was well educated and well to do. He talked a lot about going to Canada, which at the time gave me the impression that not only was Masson looking for himself, the draft board was probably looking for him too. He gave me a phone number and his home address in Denville, New Jersey. When I dropped him off on highway 89 south of Cameron, Arizona, we never imagined that someday soon our paths would cross again.

When Aaron and I finally reached Tsegi, we learned that Trader Jim had moved the old hogan I had slept in during the ride. He had taken it apart one stone at a time and put it back together in the parking lot of the trading post. It looked awful. I showed it to Aaron and pointed toward the cliff where it originally stood. He went inside and came out to ask, "Why did he move it, Dad?"

"Tourists," I told him, studying the hogan and considering the deeper ramifications. Trader Jim held staunchly to the older, simpler ways. He detested commercialism and yet, he would wring his hands greedily and whoop out loud when a busload of tourists converged upon the trading post. Is it because humans are in many ways alike, with that old stand-by excuse *no one is perfect* that enables us all to display convenient degrees of integrity? Perhaps degrees of integrity is genetic, a necessary characteristic for all survivors?

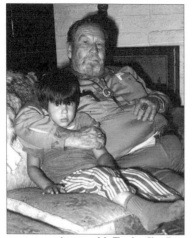 

Aaron with Trader Jim Porter and Stormy Hall in 1971.

The Council ring, the Second ring and
Stormy Hall.   📷 *js*

Aaron and I spent a few days roaming around the reservation with Trader Jim. While along with the rest of the world we had all grown three years older, things at Tsegi and the reservation had also changed. Tearfully, Trader Jim said that Jimmy Nighthawk had gone off to Vietnam and had not been heard from. Too, his earlier prediction that most of the reservation Indians would be driving new pickup trucks had come true. So, the new generation had indeed gotten their way. The last evening, during quiet reminiscing, he gave me a second ring. The only significance of the silver, turquoise and coral ring was that he had given it to me. He was greatly surprised when I showed him the Council ring that he had given to Wind Drinker and me.

Before Aaron and I left the reservation, I parked the Land Cruiser on a hill road and watched with a saddened heart as earthmovers roared and clattered in the distance. The quest for coal had grown so intense that the super shovels on Sacred Mountain had more than doubled and they were furiously digging out its holy core.

The beautiful and remote badlands of Arizona.   *js*

Jimmy Nighthawk

Came home to the reservation, no one waiting for me.
Mom and Dad have gone away, moved to Albuquerque.
Everything's just as I left it, yet nothing stays the same.
The girl I love is stringing beads, settled and changed her name.
And it gets me to thinking there's no reason to stay.
I lost my direction, when I came home today.
When I left the reservation, my folks begged me to stay.
I traded my horse for a beat-up truck, and lost my way in LA.
I climbed the hill of my childhood, to cheer when the council won.
Now they're building highways over the flats, where the
wild horses used to run.
And it gets me to thinking there's no reason to stay.
We lost our direction, when we gave it away.
Old folks pose for the tourists, their eyes seem not to see,
dust devils dancing down the street, dancing and swirling so free.
Free as we used to be.
Dancing and swirling so free.

Jefferson and Stormy. Aaron experiencing the Mojave Desert. 📷 *js*

East of Cortez, Aaron and I drove over a stream bridge and up a sandy road to find the little girl I had met in '68, but the house was deserted and there were no horses beyond the fence. Then, as I drove back over the bridge I remembered. The bridge was where she stood when I mounted Sol and rode away.

From there, Aaron and I headed northeast listening to Anne Murray's *Snowbird,* over and over, as we went to find Ray Andis, Ken Yager and more than a hundred others. Curiously, in less than three years since my ride, the once clean-faced cowboys, who used to rope hippies from horseback in the *Garden of the Gods,* had practically all become hippies themselves. I spent some time looking for Claudie, but to no avail. During the quiet times, while driving the foothills of the Rockies, she was everywhere I looked. But of course, this time it really was only a dream.

Reluctant, but convinced it was a good thing, I dropped Aaron off at my brother's in Oklahoma City. It was time for him to meet, for the first time, his Uncle John, Aunt Nadine and four cousins, John, Cindy, Mary and Patty. Then, I continued the project alone.

In West Virginia, Alvada Martin, the girl who had pawned her ring to buy me a gun, was living in a boathouse on New River near Charleston. Alvada was beautiful, married and heavily pregnant. She could not believe that I had come back to find her.

"Did you forget? I promised I would, didn't I?"

Aaron and Jefferson Spivey with Ken Yager – Phone booth where, in 1968
Spivey used his last dime to get help that never came.   *js*

Throughout most of the trail investigation, I slept out, either in the
Land Cruiser or on the ground in my sleeping bag. On many
occasions when bedding down, the parking lot of a state capitol
building was about all I could manage on the meager budget of the
project. I would awaken at sunrise, shave with canteen water and
soap, brush my teeth, comb my hair and tuck in my shirt. Then
mount the capitol steps to meet with whoever was governor. It was
that way, under varying circumstances, throughout the project. I
am sure that they all assumed I had just arrived by jet.

I secured the signatures of eleven U.S. Senators, the governors
of fourteen central states, twenty-eight mayors, Navajo Chairman
Peter MacDonald and Albert Wing, Chairman of the Ute Mountain
Ute Indian Nation.

Of all the governors who signed and affixed a state seal to the proclamation, Ronald Reagan was the only one to follow up with a letter of encouragement.

Secretary of the Interior Rogers C. B. Morton endorsed the concept, as well as Stewart L. Udall, former Secretary of the Interior, Senators Robert Dole and Barry Goldwater, along with John V. Tunney of California. Tunney made a verbal agreement to introduce a bill before Congress but never followed through. So goes it, when you are dealing with political personalities instead of patriotic visionaries. It's all show biz.

How in the world can we make money with all these people running around freely in the wilderness? Isn't Disneyland enough? We need more control!

A common problem one has when dealing with politicians is, by the time they get all fired up to do something, their term in office is up. Then, if you are really tied to your plan, you have to start all over again.

When I arrived in Washington, D.C., I was invited to speak before the National Symposium on Trails. *Time/Life* writer Sally O'Quinn, along with a photographer from *Sports Illustrated* were both present as I described the Freedom Trails concept before a huge audience using a large map of the American continent. The gathering was the first of its kind ever held. My proposal to connect the continental states with non-motorized trails, using State and National Parks as hubs for the system drew considerable interest.

I got a call from Gene Boone, coordinator for the Television Show, *To Tell The Truth,* at NBC. I agreed to make an appearance and they footed the bill. It was a short flight from Washington Dulles to Newark and from there I took a cab to the Park Sheraton on 56th $^{\&}$ 7th Avenue, New York City.

Cassette log: June 14, 1971.
Denville New Jersey is right across the bridge. The first thing after checking in, I called John Masson, the hitchhiker I had picked up at the

Grand Canyon. He answered on the first ring and we had a good laugh. We will meet tomorrow and he will drive me to studio #6 at 30 Rockefeller Plaza. Just as I hung up, the phone rang. It was Gene Boone. She wanted to take me to supper. It was late so we ate in the hotel restaurant. After discussing various aspects concerning the show, we got on the subject of books and authors. I learned she was a friend of John Steinbeck's wife, Elaine. When I mentioned John Masson, she insisted I bring him along. "We're going to need two imposters for the show." The date was set and a week later I was back again at Masson's place in my Land Cruiser. On the day of the taping, Masson was dressed in boots and Levi's with my shirt, belt and hat. The studio furnished a second imposter, also dressed like a cowboy. Then, with me dressed like a Wall Street broker, the show went on. Gary Moore was host and the panel consisted of Kitty Carlisle, Bill Cullen, Anne Meara, and Hugh Downs. All but one guessed that I was Jefferson Spivey, so I lost the five hundred dollar prize. After the taping, John surprised me by saying. "Well Jeff, I finally did it! I signed up. In a week, I'll be watching myself on *To Tell The Truth,* in some Army barracks with all my hair shaved off." He seemed happy with his decision. The following day, we bid farewell. I drove back to where I had left off and continued the trails project.

Interior Secretary, Rogers C. B. Morton signs Freedom Trails Proclamation. John Masson, my imposter on *To Tell The Truth*. 📷 Jim Aycock/ U.S. Interior Dept. & *js*

As all trails lead home, I moved back to Oklahoma City and formed the Freedom Trails Foundation on December 17, 1971.

I thought my home state would make a good pilot project for the national concept. After spending two years running up and down the capitol steps, working with the State Parks Department on a statewide trail system, very little was accomplished. The people wanted it, but the politicians wanted to make sure that it was all under their control. They finally passed a bill but no money was appropriated.

The name *Freedom Trails*, the inspirational image of the national concept, was soon abandoned. Then of course, as always when government predominates, the drive and passion went out of it. Now it is simply the Oklahoma Trails Act.

Feeling discouraged on the future of *trails* was not a thing to record and keep. Here is a moment to the contrary.

Mini-cassette log: September 1985, Santa Fe, New Mexico.
I just finished a thousand-mile ride from Oklahoma City to Santa Fe. Was interviewed by reporter William Heimbach of the *New Mexican*. I'm really depressed. Can it be that I'm the only person who wants America to have a trail system? Should I have been dealing with Hollywood all along? After all, that is where the real power lies, not in Washington, D.C. The influence of that tiny spot is the most powerful in the world. In Washington, good ideas are kept secret, in Hollywood they're made into movies. Hollywood decides the American menu, Washington merely serves it up. Gradually, the country gets in line. The individualists who really think for themselves and the dreamers that really live the dreams ultimately remain society's outcasts.
Our state and national parks are like wooded cities connecting our freeways. They are just as crowded as any city during vacation months. They are even more confining, and correspondingly, as polluted as any city on the continent. To visit some parks, reservations must be made months ahead of time.
When the chance to go is available, one will find that only the scenery has changed, the traffic remains the same. The parks are grass-less, fenced in lots with the wilderness sapped out of them. People drive hundreds of miles to a State or national park, back their trailers into cubbyholes, and pay to look at the scenery through a telescope.

So, why do we even go to the parks? For enjoyment, free of city life, to relax in a place away from the neighbors? Well now, when we enter the park gate Smokey the Bear greets everyone. Hey! Wait a minute. This Smokey is wearing a .357 Magnum revolver. Smokey has the power to put someone away for good. Smokey can invade your wilderness solitude any time he or she pleases.

"Get up; let me see your ID!"

Smokey would prefer you stay home, as far away from their wilderness kingdom as possible. The feeling I get in a national park is one of alienation. I have entered someone else's domain. I am being watched, and unable to be lighthearted. This wilderness facade is filled with uniformed guards. The supervisor is king and the rangers are soldiers, a platoon keeping everything nice and neat. This officialism as a part of the great outdoors is, unfortunately, a contradiction that may be necessary.

Two hundred and seventy-five million people visit our parks yearly. This kind of activity will eventually alter the manner in which the parks are maintained. The presence of so many people in their cars and campers makes it nearly impossible to curb the destruction. Alternate visitation will be one of the changes in the near future.

It is conceivable that some places will be entirely off limits to the public. Places such as Glacier National Park, Lewis and Clark, areas of Alaska and the Everglades. If people could migrate over a national system of trails, a crisis would not exist. The burden would be lifted and the grass would always grow. Is that so difficult to understand? Don't people know that someday our Interstate Highways will be linear cities? That I-40 will be red and green light intersections from Sea to Shining Sea?

When laws are brought about to limit the number of human births, it should be obvious that the domestic animal world will be affected as well. The larger animals will be the first put upon by such laws. Unlike cattle, horses are not considered necessities. They are looked upon as luxuries. Freedom Trails would promote respect for our national heritage and horses could remain a permanent segment of American life.

Our forefathers were wise enough to foresee the day when our open lands would be developed, so they began early setting aside land for our state and national parks. We still have the chance to update their dreams if we will – *just do it!*

I have recently been invited to SouthWest Africa (Namibia). They want me to come there with my futurist trails concept. Maybe I'll update our forefathers' dreams in Africa? Ha! That'll teach'em. But, probably not.

Currently, there are eight National Scenic Trails. Two are open to the public, the Appalachian in the East, and the Pacific Crest in the West. Only fragments of the other trails can be used. The 90th Congress approved the Trails Act on October 2, 1968, the year of my first ride, and in the same month that I arrived in Washington, D.C. It was at that time Stewart Udall, then the Secretary of the Interior, explained the Trails Act to me. 1968 is the banner year for trails in America. The Trails System Act recognized twenty-nine trails, eleven of which are National Historic Trails. The others may never be linked or opened to the public.

As most historians know, when the frontiersmen were in the process of blazing trails across the continent, they were not primarily interested in scenery. Their main purpose was to get where they were going as fast as they could via the safest and most accessible routes. Therefore, the trails crossed the least-scenic parts of the country, with wagons, railroads, and highways following their footsteps. Now, most of the old historic and heritage trails are asphalt roads and superhighways, and only sections of the old trails still exist.

The wilderness is for a special kind of person. Not special because they are better than anyone else, but because they were born with a need to be close to nature.

For a television interview in Manitou Springs, Colorado on my Canada to Mexico ride in '84, I was spiffed up, dismounted and ready to talk. There were two camera crews and two reporters. We were in Shriver Park and Ken Yager, the undoubting flagstaff of my wanderings was there with his new wife Peggy. The old telephone booth where I had used my last dime trying to get help for my horse was no longer there. The Crystal Hills Stables where Ken, Gary, and I had led Sol behind a Jeep on that rainy day sixteen years earlier was gone too. A housing community had taken its place in the beautiful hills of Manitou Springs.

In the park where we stood was the only place on the continent where my ocean to ocean and Canada to Mexico rides intersected. For some reason, the park looked much smaller than before.

Instead of duplicating answers, both reporters sat in on the interview. Here is what I said:

"Freedom Trails would have a central trail, stretching from the Pacific Ocean to the Atlantic Ocean. It would cross the Sierra Nevada Mountains, the high desert, the Rocky Mountains, the Great Plains, the Appalachians and Shenandoah Valley, the Blue Ridge Mountains and then, to the Atlantic.

"Freedom Trails would be scenic, because the concept is starting anew, seeking the most scenic areas of the country. Of course, wherever it is possible to connect portions of the old historic trails, so much the better. Unlike our predecessors, however, we are not in a hurry to get anyplace. There are numerous old military and logging roads, thousands of miles of stream and riverbeds. There are no new lands to conquer, only old ones to rediscover.

"All abandoned railroads would automatically become a part of the trails. Eroded lands and mountain passages would be utilized, because these scenic avenues have no other productive value than to inspire the human mind.

"Freedom Trails would update our park system and offer an alternative way to travel the country for people who are fed up with confining parks. The trails would be like new arteries pumping new life into the outdated park system."

At the end of the interview a small boy asked me to twirl my gun, so I did, once over my shoulder, then I spun it into the holster. A cameraman got it all on tape and that evening while watching the interview on Ken Yager's TV, the gun twirling was all that was shown. For some inexplicable reason, Freedom Trails was never mentioned. So, the only information the viewing public got from the media was that some cowboy was riding from Canada to Mexico, twirling a gun. *Good 'ole Sell'evision.*

America's youth are the losers. We have taken from them the free out-of-doors America and have given them, in return, confining cities and fenced-in freeways.

It will be more so as time goes by. Earlier generations born to freedom can moan all they please, but time will take care of that.

In the not too distant future, there will be a world so advanced that generations will spend their entire existence just trying to keep up.

I have seen America west to east, north to south and foot-by-foot. Believe me, there is a guard at the gate, and the day of the free wilderness is gone.

Freedom Trails would be a new kind of national park. The difference is the arrangement of a gigantic network of trails throughout the continent. In effect, these 'skinny' parks would reach all Americans regardless of geographic location. Our outdoor recreation system unintentionally limits access to the most mobile portion of our society. Freedom Trails would limit no one.

The truth is humans have always been fearful of nature. That is why we cloth ourselves and build walls against it. It is why we marvel at its beauty through windows of security rather than live in it, at its mercy, like animals.

Manitou Springs. Where his east & west trails cross.   📷 Mark Reis/Colorado Sun.

Tile Bottom Rivers

They're building tile bottom rivers, all across the land.
The Army Corps of Engineers, they deserve a great big hand.
Gonna level Yosemite and drain every stream.
Who cares about the scenery, we'll paint the cement green.
Gonna have pipeline-superhighways, all across the land.
Made a deal with Howard Johnson,
And our good friend Uncle Sam.
Gonna be three days a week a workin', all the rest for play.
Computers' punchin' little cards is the way we'll get our pay.
Gonna be a great new time, just you wait and see.
With the Colonel's chicken in every hand, get as fat as we can be.
Gonna be livin' in a great big bubble, with a sergeant on every
block.
And we won't have to worry,
They're gonna' keep our bubble locked.
Gonna have robot televisions, we'll put them in our trust,
They're gonna' do our baby sittin', and keep an eye on us.
They're building tile bottom rivers, as pretty as you've ever seen.
And it's all a part of the things we love,
That great American Dream.

L to R – Bill Morkel, Colonel G. J. Coetzee, Jefferson Spivey, two soldiers of the SouthWest African Special Forces and Bayard Fox.   *js*

Cowboys in Africa

The Department of Tourism and the SouthWest African Special Forces had invited me and Bayard Fox to Namibia, all expenses paid, courtesy of South African Airways. In May 1986, after an eighteen-hour flight from New York City to Johannesburg, we landed at the Strijdom Airport. Our guide, Bill Morkel, along with Ernd Roemer of SWABC-TV, was there to meet us. From there, Morkel drove his '82 Land Rover 42 kilometers to Windhoek, the small capitol city of Namibia, also referred to as SouthWest Africa. The territory is the size of Oklahoma and Texas combined. We were there to help with a feasibility study for a system of Freedom Trails and to ride across the oldest desert in the world. Bayard Fox had come along to share his expertise. His Bitterroot

Ranch in Wyoming, which borders the Shoshone National Forest and the Wind River Indian Reservation catered to trail rider's world wide.

When I first saw Bayard Fox limping toward me at the Kennedy Airport, I thought to myself, this guy was going to have trouble getting in the saddle much less ride a horse. Well I learned quickly that this man on horseback perfectly fit the old saying *symphony in the saddle*. He spoke words like yep, thankee, and pardner. Bayard was not only a real cowboy he was also a graduate of Yale.

Colonel G. J. Coetzee was the top officer of the Special Forces. He wore a straw hat and rode a white horse. Though a formidable individual, his light complexion was not one of his stronger features. His cheeks and nose were burned raw by relentless exposure to the sun. Wherever the Colonel went, his dog Boom went with him. Boom liked me a lot. A sort of kinship I'd say. The mutt was in my lap much of the time. The troopers called the Colonel, "Pinkie." Pinkie Coetzee, the Sergeant told me. At first I thought he was kidding. But regardless, being a trained Marine prevented me calling any commanding officer Pinkie!

Instead of using names, the horses of the SouthWest African Special Forces were referred to as numbers. The one I picked from a band of twenty, though possessing great conformation, was distinguished by a flop-ear. The soldiers seemed surprised at my choice of number 437, but I knew that the slim-legged gelded sorrel was the best of the bunch. Bayard rode number 960. Both were of thoroughbred and Spanish Barb mix. Each horse wore it number on the left flat of its rump, put there with some kind of hair bleach.

The Special Forces use these hardy desert animals for patrolling and for combat engagements. Seventeen soldiers accompanied us as we rode into the remote badlands. They also hunted, cooked, and made camp. We were treated with enormous regard. I even had to ask, "Colonel, mind if I saddle my own horse?"

"You want to saddle him yourself? Please do Spivey!"

From then on Bayard and I were a whole lot more independent. Hands on is what we wanted, not cared for like powder-puffs. Now, at least temporarily, we could be soldiers and it felt good.

Early one morning while eating breakfast and watching the camera crew film various aspects of camp activity, from horses snorting to the sunrise, someone turned on a radio for the news.

After a brief search through considerable static a clear station emerged. It was indeed the daily news and everyone paused to listen. Two SWAPO Camps near the Angola border had just been wiped out. I knew so little about the political problems of the country, I wasn't sure whether to applaud the event or pretend to be knowledgeable. I just nodded my head. Two days earlier, a man had been killed when his tractor ran over a landmine. North, near the Etosha game reserve, ten workers had been blown up in their VW Bus. While the news told about the bombings, no one cheered so I took on the solemn expression worn by the others.

The Special Forces have been known to attack machine gun nests on horseback, using no more than a wound-up Cobra snake as a hand grenade. One of the soldiers told me, it's like a silent bomb, and the enemy scatters in all directions.

At sunup, Lieutenant Hanna Smit led 437 and 960 over to Bayard and me so that we could saddle up. After giving them a good brushing, we led them to where the saddles were stacked on the trunk of a dead tree. By the time we had the horses saddled, the old tree stump had already been loaded into one of the supply trucks for firewood. Someone pointed out a bald spot on a distant mountain and told us to head that way, so Bayard and I, along with Lt. Smit, struck out ahead of the others.

An hour later we paused in the flats upon seeing the rest of the troopers. From where we stood, we could see forever. They were three miles behind us. The morning had started with a light cool breeze but as we neared our noon destination, it had turned into a strong hot wind. Lt. Smit took a few photographs, and then we got everything strapped down and nudged our mounts into a smooth gallop. Shortly we broke out into an earth-consuming run. It felt great, working out all the stiffness from the previous slow-moving days. I could tell that the horses were enjoying it too. Bayard and I stayed close together. Lieutenant Smit was several yards behind, running between two stringer horses. The loose horses had been trained to stay with the horses that were mounted.

At a gallop, and also at a run, I am aware of the smallest objects ahead of me. What I saw on the ground had been raced over by the others without a pause. I drew back on the reins and 437 slid to a halt and turned back. I dismounted and walked back as Lt. Smit pulled up short. I bent down and right there in front of me was a beautiful Stone Age hand-ax. It lay so shallow in the pebbled sand that its perfectly beveled edge loomed above the ground. Reverently, I turned it over, then stood up and studied it in my hand. A human being had crafted this tool, and then left or lost it, thousands of years before Jesus Christ was born. Even before the Pyramids and now, after all that history and time, I picked it up!

"A hand ax," I said, holding it out for Smit to see.

"Yes," he said, "and a very nice one too."

While Smit studied the landscape to mark the spot, I wrapped the relic in a bandanna, put it in my saddlebag and mounted up.

When we reached the Omaruru River the long hot ride was nearing its end. We followed the river for a couple more days until we got to the village of Omaruru. I reported a loose shoe on my horse, and while we were eating lunch at a place called Staebe Hotel, all the horses were loaded into trucks and I never again saw 437. Before the troopers left that afternoon, they all came into the restaurant two and three at a time to bid farewell.

After a gentle pat I handed Boom to the Colonel, then Bayard and I headed for Windhoek. Waiting was our flight to Etosha, the largest game reserve in SouthWest Africa.

In the heavy white dust coming through the windows, Morkel dug into a leather satchel behind the seat and handed me a shiny new book, titled *Bill Morkel Hunting in Africa.*

"Read it when you get back to the States," he said.

Then, once again we were hearing about the wonders and the tribulations of SouthWest Africa. Everyone was talking about independence. The government consisted of a National Assembly of sixty-two members. The Assembly and the cabinet had full legislative and executive authority over the territory of Namibia, except for matters concerning foreign affairs and defense. These two crowning principles so necessary for Namibia's absolute independence were still in the hands of South Africa.

"At present," Morkel said, "we are a country without policy. Angola borders Namibia on the north, where Cuban forces hold up a communist regime. They raid into Namibia, up north. They have East German technical advisors, you know, they're too smart to get their hands dirty. The Republic of Botswana borders the east, and south by southeast is the Republic of South Africa. West is the Atlantic Ocean, where Russian trollers move freely off shore, stealing our fish! The British, the Americans, the Germans and others are here for diamonds, uranium, copper, gold, and oil. You see! A country without policy can do very little to correct the unfairness." Morkel stopped speaking and pointed out a giant anthill packed like mud around the base of a tree. It must have been eight feet tall. He went on. "Most of the wildlife in the region was killed off. This is now farm and cattle country."

"What happened?" Bayard Fox said.

"It was quite a while back," Morkel said. "It was their way of settling the land, getting it ready for development. There were hundreds of thousands of springbok, gemsbok, kudu, and zebra. Just about everything. Killed off, like the American buffalo."

After a week in the Etosha, Bayard and I returned to Windhoek. Ernd Roemer and his TV crew met us at the Eros Airport, only a few hundred feet from the Safari Hotel where we stayed. Garard Jacques, Ambassador of Belgian and his wife Hilda, who had been with us on the Etosha tour, were there to bid us farewell.

For outsiders, SouthWest Africa is a beautiful and mysterious place. Instead of coyotes' howl at night, it is the squeal of jackals. In place of the North Star in a dark sky, it is the Southern Cross. In mid-May, when Bayard and I arrived, winter had already begun.

By now, the old discussions of independence have gone silent, for that re-occurring dream finally came true. Curiously, on my birthday, March 21, 1990, Namibia, formally SouthWest Africa became a self-governing, independent state.

Bayard Fox on 960 and Spivey on 437 pose for Lieutenant Smit.   *js*

The snap and whine of my camera invaded this bull elephant's solitude.   *js*

Najah drinking from a clear mountain stream in Wyoming. 📷 *js*

Najah

Najah was the first horse I had ever really owned. He was donated to me in January 1983. I named him after an Indian talisman that was put around my neck by Bill Boyer, during the first ride when I reached Scott City, Kansas. Boyer said it was for good luck. Long since, I had quit doubting the power of the spirits, so I was not about to take it off.

The symbol means, *In the Arms of God*. It came to America from Moorish Spain and was adapted by the Zuni tribe, calling it Naja. Earlier, before the Moors showed up in Spain from North Africa, the symbol adorned the staffs of Roman legionnaires. I suspect the symbol arrived in America on Spanish ships of the Conquistadors. I redesigned the symbol, using branches instead of the upside-down cross, which is the center post of the old design.

I received a trademark and spelled the new symbol Najah, with

a silent *h*.

Najah's registered name was Cir-Rickema. He was an Arabian Chestnut sired by Rick A Tara and foaled by Naibara Acirema on June 26, 1979. William Wederski of Fremont, Nebraska had given him to a church youth group in Edmond, Oklahoma. They in turn donated the horse to me. I changed his name to Najah.

It was 4:30 AM in early August 1984 when Steve Morland, a farrier from Guthrie, Oklahoma knocked on my door. A chill in the air reminded me that I was a month behind on starting my north-to-south ride, from Canada to Mexico. I had waited with anticipation for backing from the National Cowboy Hall of Fame. Cowboy Hall director Dean Krakel asked me to wait one more week, as the Chairman had the final say. I waited, but the season window was closing and I could wait no longer.

Morland's early intrusion did not matter because I had not been able to sleep anyway. After all, I was getting ready to add a major new chapter to my life. Leaving my wife, Allison and children, Aaron, Jeremy and Tecla for this lonely undertaking was not as light-hearted as I had hoped it would be. Though I was adding sixteen years of experience to this new ride, I was acutely aware that I was also that much older. Mike Whitaker, a friend who had wanted to accompany me on this new ride, called the night before. He had changed his mind. I was committed.

"Steve, I'd like for you to try something." I went into the garage and came out with Mr. Sol's old army horseshoes. "Just for the heck of it, let's see if they'll fit." The eighth set of shoes that I had taken off Sol sixteen years earlier fit Najah perfectly. *

Now, the horseshoes that ended the 1968 ocean to ocean ride on Mr. Sol would be the same shoes to start the 1984 Canada to Mexico ride on Najah. Who knows? Maybe Najah would walk with added spirit in Mr. Sol's hot forged, tailored made shoes.

* History of Mr. Sol shoes page 239.

Atop Independence Pass. And, no fences block railroads. 📷 *js*

Logbook: September 5, 1984, north-south ride. Flaming Gorge, near the border of Wyoming and Utah.

Last evening I camped on the crest of a foothill. It was sundown and off to the west I watched a mountain lion go to water. Off to the east was a highway with evening traffic. As the lion drank from the reflecting pool, I wondered, on which side of the hill did I belong? Then, as the highway grew brighter and the lion went up the bank and vanished in the darkness, I decided that I was right where I was meant to be.

Early this morning I heard a loud moaning. I thought someone was badly hurt. I tied my horse Najah and went to investigate. I went sidestepping down the steep bank of a ravine. To my surprise, it was a Black bear. Looked like its pelvis had been crushed. It rained last night, lots of thunder and lightning. A few yards away from where I discovered the bear, there was a large tree split down the center. Maybe it fell on the bear, or a car could have hit it. I don't remember what I said, but I used a gentle voice as I put an end to its suffering. Bless all of life's creatures.

Logbook: September 7, 1984, Jensen, Utah. I called home.

My son Jeremy, and daughter Tecla, really sounded great. Wish I could see them. Aaron wasn't there. I've seen a lot of dead animals in the last couple of days. Must be bow season. So far I've seen three antelope with arrows in them. I came upon another one today with an arrow behind its left shoulder. As I rode up, hunters drove off, their trophy covered with a tarp. I am now roasting antelope over a popping fire.

Najah and I were traveling the shoulder of a narrow mountain road; the land on either side was fenced. We were headed toward Cheffee County, Colorado, when we came upon a meadow stream that had flooded its banks and the two-lane road ahead. Though the flood had receded to the level of the road, it was still spotted with glistening pools and there was no grassy shoulder on which to ride.

Down the winding, tree-lined road ahead a car was coming. Approaching from behind was an eighteen-wheeler spraying tall sheets of water into the sky. Najah would hesitate before each puddle. And, the farther we went, the pools were larger. With his neck bowed and his nostrils blowing, he moved to the center of the road. By the roar of the truck, it was not slowing down.

I tickled Najah with a spur, but he was determined to stay on the dry areas of the asphalt. Approximately fifty yards in front of us, on a curve in the road, there was a graveled turnout. I knew we had to either make it at a run, or go for a swim. It was time to override Najah's resolve.

With a tightening bite of my spurs and the whistle of a leather whip, Najah jumped the first wide puddle as we dashed for safety. Ten yards short of our target, the eighteen-wheeler sprayed our backs and we joined the fish.

This problem arose from being too much of a softy with my trail horse when there was no danger around. Then, I saw no reason to force Najah into puddles of water against his will. "Okay! Go around." I would tell him. That was a big mistake.

Immediately after the *puddles in the road* incident when my horse nearly turned us both into road kills. I purposely began watching for more such puddles, so that I could force Najah into crossing each and every one of them. I wondered if a horse inspired the old expression, *Scared of his own shadow.*

Reflection - Manitou Springs, CO. Shriver Park is the only place on the continent where Spivey's '68 and '84 ride intersected.　🐴 Mark Reis/Colorado Springs Sun.

Logbook: October 18, 1984, Albuquerque, New Mexico.

Albuquerque is at the end of the Rocky Mountains. Should be like summer again all the way to the Rio Grande. The cold wind and snow that followed me from Santa Fe ended at the Santo Domingo Pueblo. A beautiful Indian girl named Zelda Abeita brought me a sandwich and showed me a place to sleep out of the cold night wind. Phoned Max Evans and lucky me, I was invited to stay at his place tonight. Good to have a down to earth friend who is also a world-renowned author. Met a couple of guys in Wyoming who said that they had read Max's classic novels so many times that *The Rounders* and *The Hi Lo Country* had turned to shreds. Lynn St. George, writer for the *Albuquerque Journal,* caught up with me for a story. Pat Evans will pick up my wife Allison at the airport. We will spend the weekend as guests of Max and Pat. Tomorrow I will check General Delivery mail. People are keeping up with my ride in *Horse & Rider.* Also, I'll buy a pair of Levi's and put on Najah's fifth set of shoes. They ought to last until we reach Mexico.

In 1985, I rode Najah a thousand miles to deliver a letter from Governor George Nigh of Oklahoma to Governor Toney Anaya of New Mexico, trying to connect the two capitols by a stretch of Freedom Trails. The trail would start at the 'String of Pearls' in downtown Oklahoma City and go west along the South Canadian River, using abandoned threads of old Route 66 and railroads, all the way to Santa Fe. I followed one railroad still being used from Tucumcari, New Mexico to Santa Rosa. It is not shown on highway maps, but it is there. Just west of Tucumcari, I cut through two barbed wire fences instead of attempting to cross a deeply trenched stream. Then I took a big chance on a high railroad trestle. I dismounted to lead Najah and halfway across I heard a faint but ominous thumping. The tracks ahead curved through rocky bluffs. I could see nothing. I reached down to feel the iron track. I felt the vibration and it was growing stronger.

I swung to the saddle just as the train became visible on the curve; we tore down the hard-packed railbed. We made it okay, but if all our moves had not been right, there would have been hell to pay. I was lucky and the fear I felt, I had experienced before. I should have considered my experience with the train on the first ride. Maybe we do not live and learn?

Governor George Nigh of Oklahoma. A thousand miles later, Tony Anaya,
Governor of New Mexico. *js*

Unlike Mr. Sol, Najah was not afraid of trains. In fact, he liked to run beside them. One cool morning on our way to Santa Fe, we raced a train as it picked up speed with the engineer waving us on for over a mile. The train gradually pulled away. I halted Najah and waved goodbye.

A refreshing part of the ride was when the television crew for PM Magazine caught up with me at Lake Meredith in the Panhandle of Texas. They filmed for two days and we cooked our meals over an open fire. They could tell I was living like a coyote. They always gave me the largest steak.

It was one of the toughest rides I had ever been on. It took twenty-eight days through rain and cold. On the first week out, Najah and I went down in the Canadian River, caught in coils of barbed wire buried in the river sand. I had to duck beneath the cold water and snip the tangles of rusty wire cutting into my horses' legs. Rivers are convenient-dumping places for derelict fences.

The only thing really positive about that ride was the fact that I finished it. Next time, if there is one, I'll go farther north.

Mini-cassette log: Texas Panhandle. September 23, 1985. Noon camp. This morning when I awoke and blinked at the beautiful dawn's horizon I had this bizarre vision of President John Kennedy's assassination. The image which was captured on film by Abraham Zapruder continued recycling in my mind as though my brain was on instant replay. I realized that the bullet that had struck the fatal blow, though it cannot be seen by the naked eye, is right there on the film. When computer technology becomes more advanced, an image of the bullet can then be pinpointed entering the picture, pushing and pulling shock waves in front and behind. Regardless of how granny the film is, the atmosphere on those particular frames will be greatly disturbed. It should then be obvious from which direction the bullet was fired. Ha! Then, finally the truth!

Between the good and bad, there is the boring.

Mini-cassette-log: September 24, 1985, evening camp
One thing for sure, on horseback, moving along at four miles an hour, a person has time to think. I focus on the smallest things. Today I rode three feet from a rabbit and it did not run. It just watched me go by. A large tarantula crossed my path. I paused to watch and found myself

wondering where it was headed. Maybe it was going home after a hard day. Perhaps it had kids waiting. If I didn't really need my spurs, I would throw them away. The constant grinding-ring as I walk is tough on the senses. I don't know what it is but when I am walking on a hard-packed road my boot heels make a different sound. I've tried to make them sound the same by taking longer or shorter steps, but nothing seems to work. Sometimes I think if I were just a tiny bit less sane, I would jerk them off and shoot them full of holes. I wonder how they'd sound then. Early this morning I saw a sign that read, *Real Jerky – two miles.* After seeing that sign it was impossible for me not to think about it. I rode the two miles wanting to ask whoever put it there, were they implying that one might obtain jerky that was not real? Like unreal jerky? The place was boarded up. Boy was I mad that I had read that sign. With all the grandiose world events that I was used to reading and thinking about, I rode all day foolishly contemplating that damn sign, and what unreal jerky would taste like. All the while, in my heart of hearts I knew that there was no such thing as unreal ~ ☽🌢⊗ ~. Boy, am I tired.

Someday I will tell the complete story of my Canada to Mexico ride. But now is the time to explain what happened to Najah, that great horse that went with me down the east and western slopes of the Rocky Mountain and later, hundreds of miles more.

On the night of October 17, 1988, four years after my north-south ride, a neighbor came to tell me that he had accidentally hit Najah with his car. Because of the injuries, I had to put him to sleep where he fell. My wife Allison and I were with him, as the vet worked. Najah's head was in my lap and we sheltered him from the cold mist with an army poncho. After he died, we covered him with the olive-drab poncho where he lay in the bar ditch so that my children, Jeremy and Tecla and all their friends would not see the body on their way to school the next morning.

Najah had been corralled with an electric fence. Close by was our trampoline. It attracted neighborhood kids and because they feared the fence, the night of the accident I had unplugged it.

I neglected to turn it back on, and Najah, seeking greener grass beyond, ducked beneath it.

That Najah would die in my neighborhood, hit by a car, was the last fate I could have imagined for my faithful companion of so many adventurous miles. I had trained Najah not to fear cars. I am sure he never knew to fear the one that killed him.

We had been through a lot together, crossing railroad trestles above raging rivers, being sandwiched by logging trucks on a narrow bridge. Though memories of the dangers we shared will forever loom, the good times will ascend peacefully above it all, with every sunrise.

I buried him in the pasture and used my truck to pull a large boulder down from the hill for a marker. Najah loved to run. The children watched him on their way to school, his coat shining like a penny, his tail and mane waving blond in the wind. I hope they will always remember him that way.

Spivey & Najah – The end of the Canada to Mexico ride. 📷 Carlos Rosales

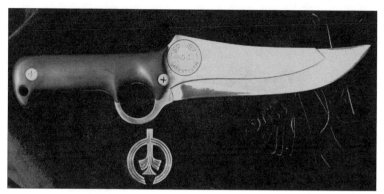

The first Sabertooth Knife.   📷 *js*

Sabertooth

When people see the knife I carry into the backwoods they immediately want one. Unfortunately, the fifteen hundred or so that I built are gone. The knife is called Sabertooth. I invented it during my '68 ride, from ocean to ocean. Necessity made me realize the kind of knife I needed. The Sabertooth is perfectly suited for wilderness survival.

The name Sabertooth was originally two words. It came from my memory of a saber-toothed skull I saw in 1965 at the Los Angeles County Art Museum built on the La Brea tar-pits at Wilshire and La Cienega Boulevard in Hollywood, California. The extinct saber tooth (Smilodon), which was a foot shorter but nearly twice as heavy as a lion, did not eat with its long fangs, it stabbed with them. It held on to its prey and used its powerful neck and shoulder muscles to pound those dagger-like teeth through the tough hide of its victim and with each violent struggle, the long fangs sank deeper. In my hand, the knife I invented reminded me of those sharp, well anchored teeth, so I named it Sabertooth.

A rock chipped to a sharp edge could very well be the oldest implement of human design. No society has existed without the tool we call a knife. It is as old as intellect and could very well be partly the cause of it. Humans may have continued walking with their knuckles on the ground had it not been for the discovery of this simple tool. A good edge is as relevant today as it was in prehistoric times. A knife has far more uses than a gun.

I used my knife for just about everything. I ate with it, dug fire pits, built windbreaks, cut rope and leather straps, sliced bread, bacon, elk steaks and stirred the stew. I drilled holes in leather belts, scraped mud from my boots and many other small tasks. There are times when one has to do things with a knife that they would not ordinarily do. Once while crossing a fence, instead of cutting the wires, I pried staples from a corner post so that I could lower the fence and cross with my horse. That of course is not something most people would have to do, unless they are traveling on horseback. With that kind of treatment, the blade of any knife will be dull the next time it is needed. Without a sharpener, streambed stones are just about everywhere and finding the right one was easy. When the grit of the stone was not right, I kept trying. It was either a grit up or grit down. In rough country, I was always able to find the right whetstone.

During my ocean-to-ocean journey, I sometimes had to hack my way down to a river, cross and then hack my way out on the other side. The knife I started my journey with was a Marble sheath knife. The blade was made of fine steel and the handle was caribou horn that had been carved into a mythical dragonhead. When my knife and gun were stolen, all I had left was a limber blade pocketknife. Because of that, I was forced to make choices I would not have made otherwise. I realized how important a straight-blade was only when I no longer had it. I brought it along because I thought it would be handy. I wanted it back because by then, I realized it was a necessity. Life in the backwoods can be difficult without a good sheath knife.

One hot day after crossing a swiftly flowing stream, no deeper than my knees in the saddle, my horse and I came out of the water in a dense patch of thorny underbrush. While hacking my way out, I tore open the skin of my knuckles to the bone. It was not a bad injury, but it was painful and that night, with my swollen hand throbbing, I visualized a knife that could have prevented the pain.

The next day, I opened my logbook and the knife I sketched eventually became a reality. I have carried a Sabertooth ever since.

While still living in Hollywood, not long after my ocean to ocean ride, I got a call from *Gun World* publisher Jack Lewis. I had just finished writing an eight-part series called "The Long Ride" for *Horse & Rider* magazine. Jack's call had not come out of the blue, *Gun World* and *Horse & Rider* were published under the same roof. "Jeff," Jack said, "how 'bout doing a story on that strange looking knife of yours?" I promptly agreed and titled the story, SABERTOOTH! Then, a month later, lo and behold, there it was, the only Sabertooth knife in existence on the cover of the October 1969 issue of *Gun World*. It did not occur to me at the time that I would ever make any more than the one I had. But Jack Lewis was getting calls and letters from all over concerning the Sabertooth. Jack advised me to get a patent, which I received in 1972. By the time my Canada to Mexico ride began, in 1984, I had built more than six hundred Sabertooth knives.

For a long while I had toyed with the notion of building the Sabertooth knife on a custom basis. I had, over time, built about four or five knives for friends. But I would never have gotten serious had it not been for Dean Krakel, Director, at that time, of the National Cowboy Hall of Fame. Years before, in 1968, at the end of my ocean to ocean ride, I had been honored by the Cowboy Hall. Before news cameras, Dean Krakel had presented me with a commemorative inscription. He was fascinated with my story and we became good friends. One morning the phone rang, and it was Dean. He had a copy of that old magazine with my knife on the cover. "Jefferson, I want to talk to you about your knife," he said and then added the magic words, "Lunch is on me."

While we ate, Dean stared down at Sabertooth # 1 and compared it with the magazine cover shot. In between bites, he turned the knife this way and that and then he finally said, "I would like for you to build a special edition for the Cowboy Hall. What do you say?"

"Are you kidding?" I laughed. "I'm not a knife maker. I'm a writer... a saddle bum. You know that!" What Dean wanted had come as a shock. I was all prepared to build one knife for him, but to instantly commit myself to such a long term project muddled my thinking.

Dean smiled. He knew I was a dreamer out of work with family to consider. "Well think it over, okay?"

That's where we left it, with my good sense telling me to grab the offer and my sense of freedom standing in the way. After two weeks of serious cogitating, along with a cold wind crying at the windows, I caved in and to this day, I'm glad I did.

Okay, I decided, it's time to hang up the gun and spurs, unsaddle the horse and become a real knife maker. I called Dean. "Dean, you know my name is on that knife," I said. "And, you know I will not build a bad knife! What I'm saying is, I can't just borrow the neighbor's tools and build knives for the National Cowboy Hall of Fame. I've got to have my own tools, understand? That means I need money up front!"

"I understand, Jefferson," Dean said, without hesitation. "Come down Monday morning, there will be a check on my desk."

That was it and there was no turning back. I was committed.

I got in touch with Bo Randall. I needed to know what type of steel to use. The legendary knife maker suggested 4130 Chromolly. "It's as good as any, and better than most," he said. "If tempered right, it will cut steel." That was all I needed to hear. I ordered blanks made to the Sabertooth design and went to work.

In time, Bo Randall returned my call. He wanted to know how the knives were coming along. As we spoke, I was working on Sabertooth #015. When I finished it, I sent it to Bo. Later, I learned that it was in the Randall Knife Museum.

I built knives that I thought people would really want to use, really make the metal ring, and not just collect. But many people who purchased Sabertooth knives locked them away. The Sabertooth is just too darn pretty to use, a collector once told me.

The Cowboy Hall of Fame Sabertooth knives which originally sold for $250 now bring as much as $1500 and more. Way too much money for me, but I'm not a collector.

I returned to the workshop one afternoon with a wooden Coke crate stacked with recently tempered Sabertooth knife blades. I had already ground the blades but there was still a lot of work to be done. One blade was cosmetically damaged. The bloodline, unique to the Sabertooth, on half the blade had been ground too deep. Subsequently, it presented an ideal opportunity to test the temper of the steel without destroying a good blade. I placed the blade flat on its side, bridging two cinder blocks with space beneath it. Then, using a two pound hammer, I hit it so hard that it rang out and leaped skyward. I ducked and it hit the gravel driveway behind me. As I examined the blade, I thought to myself, it's not too hard or it would have broken. Also, it's not too soft or it would be bent, it was still perfectly straight. Now, I determined, it was time to test the sawtooth spine. After fitting the blade with walnut handles, I found a 1 ½ inch iron pipe in my junk box and clamped it in a vise. I leaned the sawtooth slightly to start the cut and then straightened it up and sawed steadily, more than halfway through the pipe. I hit the blade on the workbench to free any loose shavings and then I drew the sawtooth spine across the palm of my hand. The double row of biangular teeth were still very sharp, no damage had been done. The flawed blade contained the perfect temper. I wanted all Sabertooth knives to be the same.

In the late 1970s to 1984 I made a hundred and ten Trail Models, using old leftover Cowboy Hall of Fame blank blades, stilled stamped with the Cowboy Hall name, which I turned into a fuller by ditching out the name with a mill. And to that, I added to the spine, a double row of biangular teeth. I cut one tooth at a time with a half-inch, half-round Nicholson file. It was the kind of work that made me shout out my praises for hi-tech.

The Cross-Country models are serialized below the cathead on the left side of the blade. Sabertooth #883, which has a black blade and stag handle, though not the last knife built, is the highest number reached from the original order of one thousand blank blades. The one hundred and seventeen blades never received either became fallouts in the initial blanking, or found homes before they got to me. Recent history shows that one blank blade, never delivered to Spivey Knives, sold on eBay for $150.00.

Over the years, some models were sold not only by the old classic store, TG&Y, but Oshman's and Abercrombie & Fitch as well. Though black walnut was predominantly used for the slab handles, other materials are ivory, cape and water buffalo horn, American elk antler, moose antler, India-stag, birds eye maple, rosewood, cherry, purple-heart, pink ivory and other exotic woods, including box elder, bois d'arc (Osage orange) and others. Moose is not good because it becomes too flexible when wet.

In a class of its own, the Sabertooth is so distinguishable that after fourteen years, when the design patent ran out, I applied for and received a U.S. trademark registration for the knife itself. I also slid the two words (Saber tooth) together and obtained a trademark for the single word Sabertooth.

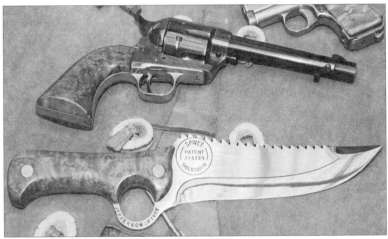

The Author's matching arms of Bird's eye Maple.

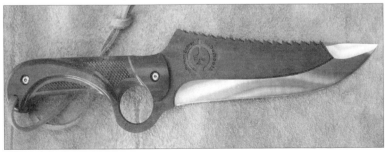

Current - Trademark Sabertooth.   js

With saddlebags, front pouch, sleeping bag and rifle boot.   📷 *js*

Cross-Country Saddle

In January 1985, not long after my north-south ride I go a phone call from Connie Egenes. John, her son, who I had helped make his own long ride in 1974 had moved from California to New Mexico, Connie told me that John was building saddles in Santa Fe. What irony, I thought. I had been looking for a saddle maker.

While John was in the Navy, cruising around in a submarine, he read about my ride and decided then that he wanted to do the same. Later we met, and later yet, we lost track of one another.

When I learned that he had started his ride, I headed west in my Land Cruiser and found him just west of Kelso, California.

After taking the load off his two animals, we built a fire. At an abandoned cabin nearby, cans of food had been left on the shelves. Someone must have known we were coming. We took over, built a fire outside, helped ourselves to a good meal and talked late into the night over popping embers.

The next morning, the two of us walked out behind the cabin and stood over a deep, wide ravine filled with boulders. In the brisk morning air, we woke up the whole countryside with our six-shooters. Actually, there was no one around. Egenes surprised me by being a better shot than I thought he would be. I showed him a few gun tricks that he could practice during the more mundane times ahead.

We then went through his pack looking for things not worth their weight. He got rid of quite a lot, including a new canvas tarp. It probably would have come in handy at one time or another, but it is prohibitive to carry an eight-pound item so seldom used.

Egenes was feeling his way. He had put himself on trial. Quite possibly, it would be the greatest test of his life. I bid him farewell and headed home.

Two months later, John phoned me from Cornfields Trading Post, near Canyon De Chelly in Arizona. He was turning back.

Incredibly, he started over again the following year. The one thing he was taking that had been a part of his first ride was his saddle. It was an old military model that had been built in Nazi-occupied Czechoslovakia around 1939. It bore the Nazi stamp, an eagle-and-swastika.

I received a card from Egenes, July 5, 1974, telling me he would reach Oklahoma City around July 18. It was later than that when he finally made it. By then, his saddle was literally falling apart. I talked the local Quarter Horse Association into buying Egenes a new saddle and together we headed for Shepler's western store. We picked a saddle that could be transformed into what was needed and in a couple of days Egenes was able to ride on. He reached Virginia Beach, Virginia, on November 1, 1974.

In 1967, at the Glenn Randall Stables in North Hollywood California, I decided that a Cross-Country Saddle was needed.

"I just work here," the man there told me. He knew I was coming; I had called before starting out.

The large gentleman led me to an old barn that had been built long before the city that had expanded around it. It was a hot day when he opened the door and ushered me inside. I stepped into the cool shade and paused in utter bewilderment. McClellan saddles were stacked along the walls and hanging from ropes in clusters.

"Wow! I've never seen so many Army saddles."

"We have more than three hundred here, about half of what we've got. We just rented a bunch to a couple of studios," he said as he started back out the door. "Take your pick. When you find what you want, bring it up front."

Like a kid in a candy store, I was literally wading through saddles, stacking and unstacking them, trying to decide which one I wanted. Most were plain trooper types, with only the seat rigging straps and regulation U.S. Army Hood Stirrups, with U.S. stamped deep in the heavy, two-ply leather.

Finally, after about an hour and a half, I settled on an officer's model, different from the trooper because of the leg pads and open brass stirrups. I narrowed it down to five saddles. From there, it was simply a matter of stitching and leather quality. The one I picked was the best of the bunch. It had all the original brass fittings, double-ply stirrup straps, and supplies hook-up rings. I traded the brass stirrups for a set with leather hoods off a trooper saddle, and then I latched onto a beautiful set of U.S. saddlebags.

When I paid for the saddle, the bags, and the stirrups, I felt a little like a thief. It all added up to $41.60, including tax. An irony is that a painting of my ocean-to-ocean saddle sold for $900 in 1975. I found out that the saddle I had picked had been used in several movies, including John Wayne's version of *The Alamo*.

The saddle was like riding a smooth log. I am sure it was originally built with mostly the horse in mind. I was badly in need of a horn that it did not have. Somewhere, near the end of the ocean-to-ocean ride, Mr. Sol decided to massage his back in a dry streambed with the saddle on. At the time, I was too far away to do much about it. The sand was deep, and he rolled completely over twice. I drew my gun and shot into the trees above him. He leaped up and ran to me like always when something scared him.

Upon close examination of the saddle, I found that the wooden tree beneath the leather at the peak of the pommel was broken. If it had not been for the built-in metal braces and the rawhide covered tree, the saddle probably would have fallen apart long before I finished the ride. That was the worst treatment the saddle received during the long journey, with the exception of getting soaked several times while swimming rivers and crossing streams.

Afterward I realize the broken pommel was a relief for my horse, Mr. Sol. The narrow rising pommel never really fit him properly. If it had, it would not have broken when he rolled on it. The saddle had simply conformed to Sol's back.

By the time I decided to ride from Canada to Mexico, I knew what I wanted in a saddle. Neither the McClellan, nor the California saddle I had would do the job. I wanted the rigging capacity and the light weight of the McClellan, but that was all.

The McClellan was designed before the Civil War and, generally speaking, men and horses got bigger but the saddle, with only a few minor improvements since the 1859 model, remained virtually the same. Too, the McClellan was not the only saddle of choice for one hundred and fifty years because it was the best in design. It was a matter of economics. There were so many warehouses filled with McClellan saddles after the Civil War that taking on just one of the many new designs could not be justified.

A couple of months before I started the 1984 ride, I took a trip to McKinney, Texas, home of the Action Company, a saddle manufacturer. After a complete tour of the place, I was given the opportunity to pick out exactly what I wanted, except for the saddletree. A McClellan tree was all they had, so I settled for it.

For good air circulation between the horse and me, I wanted the air vent (gullet) of the army McClellan, as well as the rigging. Like the Western, I wanted a covered horn and stirrup straps, but not the swells and fenders. In addition, I wanted sweat pads and saddlebags. Instead of the rigidly secured saddlebags on the old McClellan of the first ride, I developed a new design, called 'floating bags.' They are secured through the seat plates with straps that let the bags ride freely with the movement of the horse. When it comes time to unsaddle, the saddlebags, still secured to the saddle, will lay out flat and are easily manipulated.

After using this type of saddlebag hook-up for the full 3,210 miles down the Rockies, I found it an improvement over the hook-ups of the army saddle. The opportunity to design my own made it possible to have a saddle horn. To be certain that the saddle would not hurt the horse's back, I had it lined with wool.

During the Rocky Mountain journey, I found the new saddle extremely close to what I wanted, but there was one major flaw. The pommel of the McClellan-style tree was too narrow. Even with the wool lining, it did not matter how much padding I used.

By the time I reached Manitou Springs, Colorado, Najah, a trot freak, was showing some wear on his hide. Just above and behind his withers, the skin was bubbling up. Also, the rigging ring was too small. The saddle rigging leather coming together from behind the seat and in front of the pommel, along with the latigo cinch strap, was bunched up in too small an area.

I took the saddle to Bingo's Saddle Shop in Colorado Springs, and Ray Davenport, the owner, put on a new set of oversized D-rings, which made it much better than before, enabling a wide cinch strap to spread out without piling up. I was using a thick hair pad and a double blanket under the wool-lined saddle. I knew the greatest problem was the weather itself. The constant rain was mixed with the midday heat. I walked and led Najah a good deal. While leading, it became routine to loosen the cinch and pull the saddle back a few inches so air could circulate through the gullet.

Before I reached the southern border of Colorado, I acquired a therapeutic pad, adding it to the already thick layers of padding on Najah's back. Each time I saddled up, I turned the bottom pad over so that the irritation on his back was against the dry side. By the time I reached Albuquerque, the gall sores on Najah's back had healed. That saddle became the transitional for the final design.

For five months, I drove back and forth from Oklahoma City to Santa Fe, to work with John Egenes on the first saddle. When I got the chance to design a saddletree, I headed for Moab, Utah.

When Jim Perry, the owner of the Hercules Saddletree Company finished roughing out the wooden saddletree, I took it home and gave it the final touch. Mostly for cosmetic reasons, I eliminated an ungraceful stitch-line on the leather along the bottom of the bars, and designed a new type of stirrup hanger.

This set up is simple and strong. In two parts, the hanger includes a receptor bracket bolted to the saddletree with a stainless steel strap. This design enables a saddle maker to finish the saddle, including all the stitching, before the stirrup hangers are secured. The hangers are double-jointed six-gauge tempered stainless.

I was never satisfied with a rigging strap cinch ring or the common D-ring. After cutting up two large brass D-rings, I puzzled together an entirely new pattern. The center post keeps the straps from changing positions and, at the same time, leaves plenty of room for a double wrap. The new ring is molded of silicone-bronze. The handcrafted saddle with brass fittings, including fixtures for a breast strap and crupper, is finally a reality. When I want a weekend saddle, I have it. If I decide to spend time in the wilderness, I have the snap-on gear for a heavy duty rig.

Just as the McClellan was created from a calculated mixture of the Hope, Grimsley, and the Campbell saddles, I developed the Cross-Country Saddle from a mixture as well. My thousand-mile ride from Oklahoma City to Santa Fe provided an opportunity to test the new design. I went into the river on three occasions, and the seat was torn by Najah's iron shoe when he leaped over me one night during a thunderous downpour. The Cross-Country Saddle is not meant for heavy roping. Stripped, it is a pleasure saddle. Loaded, it is a work-rig for hunters, park police and border patrol.

Some saddles can be rigged for traveling, with tie-downs, hook-up rings, canteen, sleeping bag and rifle boot. A forty or sixty pound stock saddle is not meant for long distant journeys and modern saddles that are very light are too fragile to support the rigging that holds the necessary weight.

Canada to Mexico – Ratón Pass, NM. First Cross-Country Saddle design. *js*

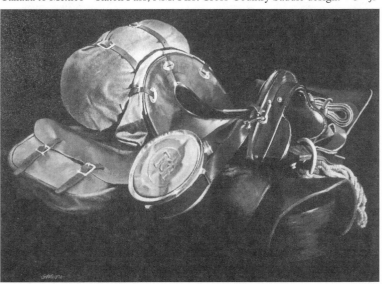

The 1968 Ocean to Ocean Saddle. Painted by Gary Myers. *js*

Part Three

Planning a Ride

The planning of a cross-country ride must take on the same importance as the journey itself. Actually, it is very exciting, the true beginning of the adventure that puts it on solid ground.

To consider making an extensive journey on horseback, with your objective weeks or even months away, the project must be the most important thing in your life. If it is not, you should wait until it is. Otherwise, unless blind luck is your guide, your dream journey may fail.

People always asked me, "Why are you doing this?" I seldom gave the same answer, yet the answers I gave were true. Sometimes there are many reasons for altering one's life. I simply grew tired of watching my friends waste precious time waiting for the phone to ring.

Instead of committing to an extensive journey right off the bat, take a friend on a two-week ride from your present location and back again. Then you will know what you are getting into.

Riding clubs are the backbone of trail riding in America. They usually prefer shorter rides, twenty-five to fifty miles and make time for such fun as music, dancing, cookouts and sleeping beneath the stars.

It is difficult to plan for and lead a group of riders on an extensive journey. Therefore, others in the group should be strong extensions of the project. Everyone must trust the judgment of others no matter how young. If there are pack animals involved or extra horses, pairing up should be worked out long before the journey begins. Once the group determines the right partners, horse to horse, and people to horses, stick with that combination.

If you're going to fish, you will need a license for each state you plan to cross, unless you're going to fish on private lakes. Even then, the situation changes from state to state. If you are making your trip alone, I doubt you will have problems fishing. If you are with a group of riders, it will be difficult to travel, camp, or fish without making arrangements ahead of time. The thing to do is contact the Fish and Game Department of each state you plan to cross and purchase licenses in advance.

Four riders on a thousand-mile ride, without any unforeseen problems, will have to move right along to finish in a month. Keep in mind, on horseback one seldom rides in a straight line. There are many side trips for water, camping, and natural barriers such as lakes, canyons and mountains. Sometimes rivers have to be forded or one must ride miles to find a bridge to cross. It should be no surprise when a thirty-mile trek becomes a fifty-mile journey.

'As the crow flies' is double the distance on horseback.   js

On a long ride, you can expect to resort to highways. Secondary roads are less traveled, but also less cared for. There are dangers: barbed wire, glass, cans, holes and drainage ditches. While freeways are usually mowed and wide they are the most traveled. So avoiding one obstacle leads to confronting another. Sometimes riding the road shoulder is the only option.

On a Missouri road shoulder   🐃 Bill Boyer

Packing

Compactness and neatness take on stronger meaning while traveling on horseback. Everything must be equally distributed throughout your backpack, saddlebags and saddle-pouch. You must treat each piece of equipment, no matter how seemingly insignificant as one of a kind, for that is exactly what it will be. Losing just one item can result in needless hardship.

The importance of keeping everything tied down and in its place cannot be over emphasized. During the north-south ride, for instance, I nearly always unbuckled my gun belt and hung the rig over the saddle horn when I dismounted to lead my horse. Before remounting, I always put the rig on, so that it would not bounce against my leg. Nothing should be flapping or dangling while traveling in the saddle.

You cannot always know the moment something is going to happen, and may need to separate yourself from your horse in an instant. Your horse may bolt in the face of danger, in which case you certainly do not want to be blinded by a flapping poncho or to be dragged by a dangling belt or lead rope.

High in the Teton Mountains of Idaho, headed southeast for Wyoming, Najah and I came face to face with a large black bear. We had seen bears before, but not like this, it was a near head-on collision. Najah went sailing over boulders, under tree branches, and down the mountain slope like a horse without a rider. The bear, as I recall with a brief glance to the rear, was doing the same thing in the opposite direction. Suddenly, I was trying to retrieve the dangling reins I had carelessly put down while digging in my backpack for a granola bar. When Najah and I finally agreed to a halt, I dismounted to check everything and to reassess my not so courageous horse.

"What a coward! Leave me with the bear, huh? You're just about ready for dog food, ya know that?"

But, nothing can scare a horse like a bear. For my own sake, I should have been more attentive. I had spotted a bear earlier in the same region. It could have turned out a lot differently. The bear and I in a treetop tussle and Najah headed for greener pastures.

An abandoned railbed south of Helena, Montana, 1984.   📷 *js*

Albuquerque, NM.   📷 Murrae Haynes

Maps & Trails

As for picking a trail, on my border-to-border ride I purchased topographic maps at the Interior Department in Denver, Colorado. The maps I used were on a scale of 1:250,000, exhibiting water wells, tiny ponds, and even the names of ranch owners. I bought enough of them to cover the full length of the Rocky Mountain chain from Canada to Mexico. Each map shows a landmass of one hundred and twenty miles east to west and approximately sixty miles north to south.

While maps show streams as thin as a trickle, there is no guarantee that the indicating blue line will in reality be water. There are maps with a much closer view of the continent, but a closer view means more maps to carry.

The maps I carried were my personal choice. Twenty miles a day is a good unhurried ride. This gives one time to break camp in the morning and make camp in the evening while it is still light. Saturdays and Sundays should be days of rest to wash clothes, make future preparations and to check gear and horses. It is a good time to lay low, as too many people are on the roads and occupying parks and campgrounds.

Increments of twenty miles can be marked on the map to indicate a day's ride. Whenever feasible, put the end of the day's travel near water. It may be necessary to add or hold back a couple of miles for the sake of water, but it will be worth it. Weekends can be marked as major campsites.

The maps I needed but could not carry I mailed ahead to major campsites. I wrote on the package of maps, General Delivery. The main post office of any town or city will usually hold General Delivery mail for ten days. In my case, when they read – *Hold for man on horseback* – they made an exception.

On the north-south ride, I knew that I wanted to stick to the eastern slopes down the Rocky Mountain chain. The eastern slopes stay warmer for the longest part of the day. There is not enough time for the sun to warm the canyons and lower mountains of the west before it goes down. This was especially true when I started my '84 ride in late August, a month later than originally planned. I started just inside the Canadian border at the Waterton entrance and headed south. One cannot hold staunchly to any particular trail. In fact, the north-south ride was so unrestricted I found myself a hundred miles west of the Continental Divide, traveling across portions of Idaho and Utah I had not planned on.

Study your map and whenever possible ask questions about what kind of country lies ahead. If you have two gallons of grain in the morning, feed your horse half on the spot and carry the rest for evening camp. Try for two rest stops during a day's ride. While you rest, day or night, let your horse graze. I always kept the reins tied together so that I could unsnap either end from Najah's bit and hook one end to my belt loop. In this way, I could nap while Najah grazed around me. If he were frightened, I would be alerted by a sudden jerk and ripping of my belt loop.

We become lost because of things we leave undone. It is not that complicated. In times past we used stars, sun, prevailing winds, landmarks, and vegetation. But times change and the best now use computers and satellites. Even at that, on horseback, there are no guarantees. Each day presents a new plan with a new list of rules.

Find your way as would a stream, the trail of least resistance.
Love all you see, it will be there only once.

Trail Horse

I have always treated my horse with the same respect as I would a person. An equestrian must recognize that this four-legged critter can get up feeling bad just like a person. A horse gets sick and hungry. Its back hurts and its legs get stiff. A horse even gets tired of seeing a rider approach with halter in hand. If a horse knew how much stronger it was than a person, humans would not have a chance.

Like a kid, my horse Najah never liked getting his face washed, but I could tell he felt better after it was done. Being aware of the little things makes a long ride easier for horse and rider.

The curiosity of some horses, especially young ones, and the absolute lack of curiosity of others has always been a great curiosity to me.

Najah did not mind being surrounded by eighteen-wheelers revving their engines at a truck stop. Yet, in the wilderness, in the near silence, a tiny leaf moving in a breeze across our path made this experienced trail horse bow his neck and point his ears with fearful anticipation. When I told him it was okay, he would begin to relax. Obviously, horses see things differently than we do. We look ahead with intellect; they look ahead with instinct.

Connie Cole worked with Sandspur Arabians in Scottsdale, Arizona. By the time I received Najah, I had already begun communicating with Connie and other Arabian horse owners looking for the right horse for my Canada to Mexico ride. Connie had a young racehorse she wanted me to take. His name was Firefeather. He was tall and beautiful and I could not turn him down. I borrowed a truck and trailer from Mark Mayo, top cowboy on the Crown Ranch northeast of Beaver, Oklahoma and headed for Scottsdale. When I brought Firefeather home, I soon discovered the mistake I had made.

While mounted on Firefeather and going at full gallop over a wide pasture, a bald spot appeared on the ground in front of us. Firefeather leaped to one side and together we went sprawling. My left leg was caught beneath him, but only for an instant. When Firefeather rose on all fours, I was still in the saddle, but my hopes for a great trail horse had been scattered behind us. I could not trust my life to this horse. Perhaps I should have known. As always, hindsight revealed the truth too late. Firefeather, I realized had spent his life running a man-made unbroken track. Running over brushy, natural terrain was completely alien to him.

1983 Spivey and Firefeather. A racehorse not a trail horse   *js*

If you ride an Arabian horse there is one thing you can count on. Not always, but almost always, the Arabian horse is fearful of water. It's genetic, I suspect. Being a desert animal assuredly dictates the essence of the breed. Water must have been really scarce during their evolutionary development.

Perhaps to an Arabian horse, a pool of water looks like a hole in the ground. It does not match up with the surrounding terrain. Perhaps the mirrored images of clouds or its own reflection in a pool is baffling to its senses. All the Arabian horses I have ridden were afraid of water. This is not to say that the breed cannot handle water. It most assuredly can.

Once my horse entered the water, he became a porpoise with legs. Probably because he wanted to hurry up and get out. I doubt that the fear of water is unique to the Arabian, but it is definitely one of the breed's most notable traits. Any trail rider should seriously consider a test for the horse, Arabian or not, he or she intends to use on a long ride.

Traits that are inherent in the Arabian horse are essential for the backcountry. The most important are stamina and eating habits. The Arabian will eat just about anything that grows and being a desert animal it can go long periods without water. I use the Arabian horse for exactly what nature intended.

A person who is good with a horse is usually a good outdoorsman with a built-in sense of awareness to what is going on around, day or night. A rider who keeps his eyes on his horse will stay abreast of what is happening over a wide range ahead. When a horse suddenly points its ears straight up and turns them one way or another, the animal is not only listening, but is pointing straight at the source of interest.

A good trail horse is a versatile animal. It will lead, pack, or follow. Aside from that, it will make every attempt to investigate new surroundings, especially those areas where there are other horses. A rider should never let his horse rub noses with horses in new areas, especially beyond a fenced pasture. After two horses have rubbed noses over a fence, they quickly become friends or enemies.

Either way, the meeting could be disastrous for both. Biting, pawing and kicking are the usual way of enemies and, if a foal is near, a fight over or through a barbed wire fence can become a vicious sight. When the meeting is friendly, there is still the possibility of one horse contracting a virus transmitted by the other.

On my '68 ride, Mr. Sol and another horse got into a kicking match. Both horses suffered severe bruising, skin and muscle lacerations on that short encounter. My horse did more damage as he was wearing steel shoes.

Before the 1984 ride, part of Najah's training was to get him used to inconsistency. I would get up in the middle of the night, lead him out of the barn, and tie him up short in some place he had never been before. The only consistency necessary for a man and horse is a constant and absolute trust in one another.

When it comes to food, consider the geographical location and season. Most of the time, a horse will have more eating advantages than the rider will. At least a horse can eat the natural foliage. In a desperate situation one can hobble a horse and turn him loose at night so he can fend for himself. Never hobble your horse in bad terrain. Ravines and canyons have killed many a horse hopping around in the dark with hobbles buckled to their legs. I usually tied Najah on a twenty-five foot leash. I lost it and was given a quarter-inch hemp rope about twenty feet long by Preston Smith of Jensen, Utah. I still have it.

On the trail, it may be necessary to tie your horse on a long rope. A few minutes later you may find him struggling on the ground all wrapped up like a mummy. Chances are his legs will have rope burns. This is common with an inexperienced horse.

After doctoring your horse's rope burn, do not wait too long before giving the rope lesson again, using the same rope. Any discomfort a horse may suffer will be in vain if the teacher does not respond immediately to the problem in just the right way. If the hurt is bad enough, the horse will remember. Eventually the lessons-to step in and out of a coiled rope, or stand still when caught will be learned and remembered.

It would be a good to use shipping boots or leg wraps as well as a soft rope. The second time, give the animal a chance to finish its lesson. This philosophy is used when a youngster is thrown from the saddle. No matter how it hurts, get up and try again. This is for the kid's sake, to diminish his or her fear of horses.

An equally valid reason for getting immediately back in the saddle is to let the horse know that it cannot get away with getting its way. If the horse throws a rider and that individual walks away, the horse will then know it has the power to do it again. If your horse gets what it cares about most in life, you will spend all your time chasing it from one eating spot to another.

A year before the Canada to Mexico ride, I tested a new idea. With a rocky pasture void of edible grass, my horse Najah would stretch his neck over the electric fence trying to get at the thick plush grass of the surrounding yard and property. I think he knew just how to get me on a guilt trip. He only acted this way when he saw me outside. The bad part was it worked.

One day, weary of staking Najah out from one grassy area to another, I rationalized if I were to tie his rope to a cinder block he could then pull it slowly and graze over the full yard at will, without further assistance. The 40-pound concrete block would be restraint enough to keep him from running away. It seemed like it might work but I would never know until I tried it. So, I did. Five minutes later, while sitting at the dining room table, I heard a loud thud. Najah streaked beyond the window with the cinder block bouncing after him. I rushed out the back door just as he rounded the corner of the house with the cinder block swinging out like a wrecking ball behind him. After taking a huge bite from a corner of my workshop and splintering the driveway light pole, the cinder block, missing me by inches, hit the driveway three times and broke apart. Najah continued up the road at a dead run. When he finally realized he was free of the monster behind him he slowed down. Then, still blowing with relief, he went on doing what he was best at, sampling the neighborhood grass.

I was grateful that all was again back to normal and with a half dozen admiring kids tagging along, I led Najah home.

"Scaredy cat!" I grumbled. "You, from Canada to Mexico?" But of course, it was indeed Najah that I rode.

Obviously Najah had thought that the cinder block was alive, a predator, stalking him. Each time he moved it followed and the process accelerated. Now we know! These gallant steeds we entrust our lives to can be frightened by anything that moves, with the exception of someone coming to feed them. I have yet to see a horse fearful of a bucket of oats. So! A moveable stakeout is not a good idea. *Nothing ventured, nothing gained.*

On a long-distance ride there is no way to guarantee feed for your horse. You can carry a small amount of feed from time to time, but without a pack animal, two or three gallons are the limit. You might find some feed company willing to put out feed ahead of you along the trail. Get some rancher or farmer to hold it for your arrival. A friend with a pickup truck with hay and grain can be a backup. If you have none of these options, then each day, for food and water, you and your horse are on your own.

Sleeping under the stars is not as romantic as one might think when actually doing it. Changing ones lifestyle from the known to the unknown can indeed be shocking to the senses. But traveling on horseback can be the adventure of a lifetime, for the reality of such a ride becomes the mental and physical design of one's own making.

I was fourteen years old and sitting on the bare back of a lanky range horse near Sayre, Oklahoma, when told the following story.

: In Egypt, a spring herd of more than three hundred horses were running at full gallop. It was the hottest day of the year and groups of riders kept the herd in a tight column moving in a giant circle. The circle was in a place that had been picked for this event, because the low area contained the deepest sand. The horses were all Arabian purebloods and they were kept moving at a muscle-rupturing gallop for much of the day.

: Near evening, the horses were driven to an area a quarter-mile from a watering place. At this point, the horses were free to go on their own. The first horses to reach the water's edge were met by a bullet from a sharpshooter's rifle. Of the herd that was left, tribesmen were put in charge of ten horses each.

: One year later, in the same place, the ritual was repeated with the same horses. This time, however, each animal had been trained for a year. An important aspect of their training was to come at a call. At day's end the herd was driven to the water's edge. Then, just as the thirsty animals lowered their muzzles to drink, the call was sounded. Most of them instantly retreated, dashing back to their master's call. The few that remained were shot where they stood. The horses that passed the test of their bloodline became honored members of the tribal family with tents equal to those of their masters.

When the old man finished telling me the story, he squinted into my eyes, winked and rode away. I got the feeling that he had seen it all happen.

I will admit, when I chose an Arabian horse for my ride, the story of the Egyptian horses did influence me a bit. The coast-to-coast ride strengthened my faith in the breed that carried me again in 1984 from Canada to Mexico. This is not to say that other breeds do not make good trail horses. I have met individuals over the years who would not think of riding anything but a well-trained mule into the backcountry.

I have come to know that the success or failure of any long ride rests in the hands of the rider himself. An exceptional horse will of course be a plus. Riding one that is not as good means the rider must know how to compensate. I was fortunate to have had good horses on all my rides.

The best of any horse comes out in the gelding.

A good height for a trail horse is fourteen and a half to sixteen hands. For a long-distance trail horse, size begins to go against itself somewhere beyond sixteen hands. The bigger the animal, the more food and water it will need.

Picture in your mind a wild mustang. Its size, hardiness, and agility are just about what you are after. Before the 1968 ride, I considered a mustang, because I never dreamed I could actually have an Arabian. Unfortunately, people do not fit into the ways of a wild full-grown mustang. It would be difficult to properly train one without taking away his most valuable attribute, the very characteristics that made you want him in the first place. If you raise one from a foal, you would end up with just another horse, which may or may not be what you are after.

Between five and ten years old is best, though you can allow a bit either way. Mr. Sol was four and a half years old when we started the ride; Najah was five. I prefer a young horse; putting up with the curiosity of youth is well worth the energy and strength.

A horse definitely needs to be shod. It is better to have tailor-made shoes for your, but sometimes hot-forged shoes are hard to come by. The types of shoes depend on the overriding terrain.

In the mountains you need digging-in ability. Shoes with a minimum of one-quarter-inch cleat toes and heels are best. In flat country, this is not necessary, but for all-around trail riding, your horseshoes need holding ability. Of the five sets of shoes that Najah wore, only the first set had been hot forged. Most anyone would prefer hot-forged shoes for their horse because the shoes are individually fitted. The store bought kind can be bent to fit. They are easier to come by and less expensive, but not what I prefer.

The concern you have for your feet should also apply to your horse. The protruding heel of a horseshoe can be caught in barbed wire, a board on a bridge crossing, or any number of things on the path. A horse's foot can literally be jerked from its socket. If a horse throws a shoe and it cannot readily be replaced, avoid muscle rupture by getting rid of the shoe on the other side. When hooves become brittle, pack them with grease or stand the animal in shallow water whenever possible, like a manicurist soaking fingernails.

Identification for your horse is for your sake, in the event it runs off or is stolen. I prefer a photograph that I can put in plastic and carry in my daypack. The old method was a blank bill of sale with a profile drawing and penciled-in markings of a particular animal.

On the trail, some horses can get along better than others eating the natural foliage. When Najah could not get grass or grains, he ate leaves, weeds and flowers.

The hot-forged shoes of Mr. Sol ended the ocean to ocean ride. Sixteen years later, Najah started the Canada to Mexico ride with the same set of shoes. 🐴 *js*

My ocean-to-ocean mount, Mr. Sol, died in 1983. About a month before I began the ride from Canada to Mexico, I telephoned George Rosenberg, Mr. Sol's owner. I wanted to tell him of my intention of riding down the Rocky Mountain chain. And, I wanted to know how Mr. Sol was getting along.

"Jeff," he said, "Mr. Sol is dead. He died last winter and I tried to let you know, but couldn't get you." In a moment of silence, I thought of the last time Sol and I were together. It was at the Arabian Horse Show in Oklahoma City. That once dapple gray Arabian had turned completely white. Each day for a week in the arena spotlight he was given a standing ovation. Though it had been a great honor and a fitting farewell, all that glitter now seemed at odds with what we had done.

"Did he go easy?"

"I think he did," George said. "There was no broken grass or scarred ground. He went down and that was it. He was twenty you know, and prone to colic."

Near Shoals Indiana.   Bill Boyer

Mr. Sol

Let's go Mr. Sol, to where the grass grows tall,
the good life is waiting us there, sun shining everywhere.
You may never know, why stars above us glow,
the reason the sun drifts away, but you will feel
love everyday, in the words to you I say.
Someday, Mr. Sol, I will recall, over and over again,
seasons as free as the wind.
Destiny knows how far we must go.
Though visions of love swiftly fly, we'll not leave this moment to die,
keep it in your eye.
Let's go, Mr. Sol, to where the grass grows tall,
the good life is waiting us there.

Together for the last time, Spivey and Mr. Sol appeared at the Oklahoma City, State Fair Arena – Oct. 24 to 29, 1972.   The Daily Oklahoman

If you really trust your horse, there is no sense in training all day in a circle. Do it on the trail. Saddle up and go! However, do it gradually and use the lightest saddle you have. It should be in good condition and preferably one that has been used often on the horse you plan to ride.

Get aboard your trail horse and head for the countryside. Watch your mount's reaction to everything, especially cars and trucks. Look for backwoods trails and stay away from deep ditches along secondary roads. Give him a chance. When you are ready, you both will meet the challenge.

An equestrian is always vulnerable, and at the mercy of people, nature, and all the elements. The trail rider must choose his equipment carefully. Hooded stirrups offer more protection from the rain, heat, cold and thorny brush. Chances are slim that a boot foot ever would slip through an open stirrup. However, some riders do not wear boots. Closed stirrups, such as the bull-nose, monkey-nose or the fancier pigeon-wing are slightly heaver than open stirrups, but are worth the extra weight on a long ride.

It is unwise to trot or even walk a horse along a barbed wire fence. Without covered stirrups, the sheer weight of a moving horse can cause severe damage to a rider's foot. Besides shielding off water and snow, covered stirrups provide a little more cushion on the horse's sides while saddling up.

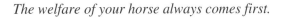

The welfare of your horse always comes first.

U.S. Cavalry stirrups.   📷 Bill Boyer

1985 Oklahoma City to Santa Fe. *js*

Tack & Day pack

New tack should be broken in before hitting the trail. I once was told by an old cowpuncher that the first thing to do with a new saddle was to throw it into a water tank and let it soak over night. "The next mornin'," he said, "cinch it up tight and ride it till it's dry. It'll be the best fittin' saddle you ever rode."

There is merit in part of the scheme, the part to mold the saddle for a better fit but water is never good for leather. If a saddle gets wet let it dry out slowly in the shade. So, what's the big hurry to break in a saddle? I don't see any mavericks running loose.

The best way to break in a saddle is simply by riding it often and keeping it well oiled with good leather conditioners.

The worst thing for leather is not using it.

Starting a long ride with a forty-or sixty-pound stock saddle is not a good idea. A saddle should not be much heavier than that with all the supplies hooked to it.

It is okay to start out a little heavy. It's a natural thing to do. You can dump just about anything but your saddle. It is easy to get rid of an item, but when you need something and do not have it, it will be hard to come by when you are roving on horseback. I jettisoned a number of items as I rode. One thing for sure, there will be time to decide what is needed and what is not.

A good sleeping bag is the best way to go. However, a lightweight down-filled bag is expensive. The mummy-type I strapped behind the saddle weighed two pounds and cost around two hundred dollars. It is reversible and is better than a blanket at keeping out bugs and other unwanted critters. When it comes time to saddle up, you simply stuff the sleeping bag into a short, tube-like pouch and strap it down behind the saddle seat.

When Najah and I reached Meeker, Colorado, Billy Holmes was good enough to put us up for the night. A close friend of Billy's, a highway patrolman by the name of Larry Coffman, brought Najah a sack of grain. On the cold rainy morning of the following day, Larry caught up to me just as I mounted up. To my surprise, he handed me a small gift covered with a bread wrapper.

"It's a tent," he said. "I guarantee you'll need it. Just slip it in your backpack, it won't add much weight."

Neat fellow, I thought as I rode away. It was not long before I learned how right Larry was. It rained to drown the devil that night and the six days and nights that followed.

I had always slept beneath the stars, in an abandoned barn, in or under whatever I could find. The tube tent, made of polyethylene, was about nine feet long and eight feet in circumference. It was very useful when I was able to find a place to tie it up. It weighed about two pounds and it was definitely worth taking. Mostly, I used the tent in heavy rain and snow. Both ends of the tent were open, but I could slide in my gear and collapse the ends to keep out the elements. Once, I hung the tent to a fence using my reins and the snaps on either end to hold it there.

1968: A lakefront campsite in Ohio.   1984: A picnic table in Utah.   *js*

A daypack for a long horseback journey is a necessity. It is tough becoming accustomed to a pack. I wore it all the time except in difficult situations like leading my horse up a mountainside. A daypack is the smallest of the backpacks. It is just right for a person on horseback. If it were any larger, it would drag against the saddle seat, making life in the saddle very uncomfortable. A daypack can carry all the necessities for the equestrian.

The nylon material used in building the pack is so tightly woven that it lacks ventilation. Even with a cotton shirt between you and the pack, you may break out with heat rash in the first or second week of a ride. The rash may subside after your back becomes accustomed to change, or it may not. It depends on the heat of the day, the dye and the density of the material used in your shirt. During the '68 ride, the weather was very hot and my legs became badly chafed.

It was mid-July and I was wearing a new pair of Levi's. I paused long enough in some small town to run them through a washer a couple of times, which seemed to help. Three days later, the rash was gone.

After the first week of the Canada to Mexico ride, I developed heat rash on my back. All I could do was ignore it. I took off my backpack more often and it finally went away.

Try not to start a ride with new equipment, especially clothing, boots or backpack. Many companies specializing in outdoor equipment sell outer garments made of Gortex that ventilates and sheds water as well.

My pack was an intricate part of my daily dress. It was a small joke when I mounted up to say; 'I carry the backpack so my horse will not be burdened with the extra weight.'

1968 Logbook.   *js*

216

js

Medical

Most medicine, external or internal, that works for you will work for your horse. Just make sure when you start out that your mount has been vaccinated for tetanus. Worming should be done every two months. To guard against flu or other possible respiratory problems, immunize against influenza and encephalomyelitis. Vaccines are available in a combined form that includes tetanus, so one injection covers all three. Follow up the initial shot in three weeks, and get a yearly booster.

If immunization is current, a booster shot is all that's needed. A vet may recommend vaccinating against rhinopneumonitis too. Ivermectin is the generic for what is needed to kill bots and other internal parasites that are the greatest threat to health and performance.

On my first ride, Mr. Sol cut his left rear foot just above the hoof when he jumped a fence. That cut became a major concern. It had my close attention for all the time it took to heal, open and reheal.

Medical attention is scarce in the wilderness. There is always the threat of sickness and death.

I was high in the mountains when my tooth became abscessed and there was no help to be found. For me, it was sleepless in the Rockies. All night I lay with my jaw pounding and my face hot with fever.

At sunup the pain was unbearable. My jaw felt like it was being hammered with a chisel. I got angry. The upper right molar had to go. While psyching myself up, I went about my usual chores. I hung my sleeping bag in the sunlight to dry and stirred up the fire. I had lost my fishhooks and tackle, so there was no string to use. The leather chinstrap on my hat was too thick and the buttonhole on my shirtsleeve was too bulky to hook over a tooth. I dug into the saddlebag for my long-nose pliers.

I knelt on a flat boulder at the edge of a cold rushing stream and cleaned my wire cutters by jabbing them into a mound of sand. I opened my mouth and guided the pliers to the bad tooth and gripped down hard. I pulled steadily, harder and harder. I could feel and hear the tissue tearing away from the root. But the pain was too intense and I released the tooth. With a moan I leaned over and splashed ice-cold water into my mouth, but it didn't help. It made me shiver more in the cold air.

Tears rolled down my face as I clamped down on the tooth again. With a deep breath and my eyes shut tight, I snapped my head up and gave a quick jerk. I opened my eyes and there, in the grip of the pliers, was the largest tooth I had ever seen. Wow! I thought that's more than just a tooth. After close examination, while blood gushed into a wadded-up T-shirt, I realized that a tiny bit of my gums was attached to the root. Immediately the fever subsided. After a good rinse with salt and stream water I felt much better. By the time I broke camp and saddled up, the pain was completely gone. I actually felt good and I was ready for a great new day.

Dangers

*Of all the creatures that roam the continent, the most dangerous
and unpredictable are bears and humans.*

Many women have asked for advice. Never ever go to the deep
wilderness during a menstrual period, especially in bear country.
Black bear and grizzlies are known to maul and even kill women
who camp out in this condition, ignorant of a bear's natural
instincts. The bear is a dreaded enemy of both horse and rider.
However, bears are never looking for trouble; food is their only
concern. Go easy, chances are a bear will do the same. Be wary of
trout streams and berry patches in bear country.

Find roads with shoulders wide enough to be safe from traffic.
Set out preconceived campsites about twenty miles apart. It can be
a semi-wilderness campsite or a nice warm farmhouse where
someone will be expecting you and your horse, and provide feed
and whatever else you might need. I think the latter is the best
notion for a first attempt at a long-distance ride.

No matter how far the equestrian retreats into the wilderness,
there are always jokers and bandits around.

Trucks and cars have a tendency to treat the equestrian as though
they too are machines with all the same protections, such as brakes
and metal shells. Unfortunately, a man on horseback is at the
mercy of a mechanized world.

Some drivers are curious to see what will happen to the horse
and rider when they honk, rev their engine, or create a backfire.
Often this will happen at the worst possible time, like when the
rider is crossing a bridge or has been caught at a crosswalk. When
a horse is not familiar with cars and traffic, it is best to skirt all
towns, ideally by less used dirt roads.

Make camp in an empty pasture and if possible, out of sight
from travelers on roads and highways. People will lead away or

run off a horse just for kicks. The rider then is stranded and his horse is somewhere on the loose and in danger. Be watchful of overly friendly or curious people. When weather permits, make camp in an open area. Take advantage of a clear vision all around.

Snakes are rarely a threat. The only snake that ever attacked me was a western racer. I was in the saddle and Najah was going at a fast walk and suddenly, the unusually long snake slithered at us, lifting its head high in the air, as high as my stirrups. This had never happened to me before. I was taken completely by surprise.

I reined Najah away from the pursuing snake and kicked out with my stirrup. The racer fell back gracefully, but rose up again, higher this time, and came at our rear. The fact that the snake was non-poisonous did not instantly come to mind. Otherwise, I may not have killed it. It all happened so fast and I acted on instinct. I drew my gun and blew its head off. I considered it a very rare occurrence.

I would never kill a snake unless it is necessary. Contrary to popular belief, a rattler will not always warn you by rattling. It may not rattle when it is shedding, just had a heavy meal, or when it is caught dozing. If your knowledge of herpetology is not up to distinguishing any of these conditions, remember that rattlers must neither coil nor rattle in order to strike. Beat the bushes and walk around the area where you intend to camp. Make the place uninhabitable for anything but yourself. When critters learn that you are there they will stay clear.

During the 1984 ride, two logging trucks tried to catch Najah and me on a narrow bridge in the high North Country. The trucks came at us from the north and from the south. One was loaded with logs and the other was empty. I had to spur Najah into a dead run to clear the end of the bridge as the trucks roared by, blowing their air horns. Najah lost his footing and we went sliding in a bar ditch filled with ice-cold water.

One of the most memorable moments of the 1984 ride was when I drank bad water and fell sick from the saddle. The Huttorites of the Milford Colony near Wolf Creek, Montana, found and cared for me as one of their own. They made my stay a grand occasion.

They all dressed in dark suits and hats, white shirts and string ties and came forward one at a time to meet me. The Elders came first. Each shook my hand and then the young ones followed, fascinated by my presence. On my first ride, I spent a couple of days with the Amish in Indiana. The Huttorites were similar, but different.

They owned machinery, trucks and farm equipment, all very modern. Their milk storage tank of polished stainless steel filled a large spotlessly clean room, and I am sure there were other lifestyle differences not as pronounced. I gave my harmonica to a boy who rode with me the day I left. The song I played, *Beautiful Dreamer*, captivated him. He promised he would learn to play.

Phillip Wipf. I gave him my harmonica.   *js*

From the emptiness of Wyoming to the friendly crossing in Albuquerque. *js*

Canada to Mexico. 📷 *js*

Guns on Horseback

The single action revolver is a simple mechanism, compared to more complicated guns. There are fewer parts to consider when it has malfunctioned. More than one hundred and fifty years of success can be attributed to its straightforward cock and fire, hammer and wheel operation. If you lose a firing pin, you can replace it with the end of an eight-penny nail. If a hammer spring breaks, a rubber band wrapped around the front of the ejector housing and over the hammer will work. If a locking-bolt spring breaks, one can hold the cylinder in battery and still fire the gun. Chances are slim that these measures would ever be needed, but improvising can sometimes be a necessity in survival mode.

A rubber band replaces a broken hammer spring. Survival tools. *js*

I purchased my first .45 Colt while working in a gun shop at the age of thirteen and I have had one or another ever since. At the same age, I learned to cut down .410 shotgun shells that would fit in my .45 long Colt revolver. With a good tight crimp it is a good shell at close range and the longer the barrel, the farther out the pattern of buckshot will hold together. One morning in Arizona, I awoke to a gathering of doves at a government water tank. They were gravelling-down pebbles for their digestive system. Three rapid shots of the .410 put up a wall of buckshot that downed two for breakfast. The three rapid shots were accomplished by raking my thumb and middle finger of my left hand over the hammer of my Colt. It can be faster than an automatic pistol but it takes time and a good deal of practice to master with confident and accuracy.

I doubt that anyone had ever fired a gun around my horse Najah before I got him. He was gun-shy. I knew that I had to take care of that problem before making a cross-country ride. I started out with a .22. Pretending to ignore Najah, I would walk into the pasture and pause about twenty feet away, turn my back and fire at the ground. Each day I got closer and finally he began to accept the loud bang. One day, I turned in the saddle and fired at the ground behind me. Najah's head snapped up. His ears twitched with anticipation, but I put the gun away. The next time I fired six rounds straight down at the ground. The .45 came next and Najah was less mindful of the .45's boom than of the .22's sharp ring.

Logbook: August 21, 1968. Nearing St. Louis.
Very hot, hot, hot. Can't stand this heat. Can hardly walk, my legs are burned raw. The sun makes me dizzy. It's burning right through me. Was stopped by Highway Patrol for carrying a gun. I showed them a letter from Governor Warren Hearnes and all smoothed out. Politics!

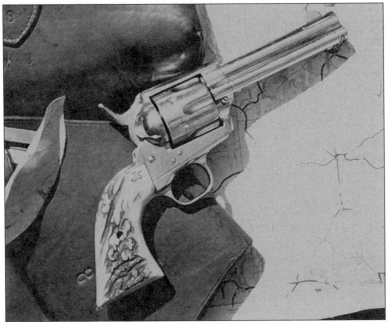

This Colt .45 with JS on the handle was stolen on Spivey's 1968 ride.　　js

The gun stolen from me in East St. Louis was a second generation Colt. It was made 1959-60. It was nickel-plated, the handles were stag and my initials were carved on the right grip. With a magnifying glass against a color slide of me holding the gun, the somewhat blurred serial number appears to be 27783SA. The .45 Long Colt is powerful enough to knock down any living creature on the American continent. Admittedly, the illustrious history of the Colt Single Action Army is partly the reason I have always carried one. Too, much of my time, the gun enabled me to pay the bills while teaching actors and would be actors the art of gun handling, along with gun safety to law enforcement groups.

The pretty daughter of a coalminer pawned her ring to buy me a gun. Alvada Martin was afraid that something might happen to me without a trusty six-shooter at my side. We went to a pawnshop in Charleston. The shop had no Single Action Colt so I picked out a .32-20 Smith & Wesson. The S&W was military issue and stamped on the sideplate with either a Spanish or Brazilian crest. The gun was in perfect mechanical condition with a six-inch barrel, walnut grips and a lanyard ring on the butt. Alvada's father, Arnold, was the owner of the Kanawha Forest Stables. They put Sol and me up for a week and before I left, they surprised me with a much-needed new pair of boots.

When I reached Washington, D.C., I was asked to appear with my horse at the International Washington Horse Show, the largest horse event in the country. The Royal Canadian Mounted Police gave me a place to put my horse and gear in their tent. When I returned after supper to check on my horse, I learned that the gun Alvada had pawned her ring for and given to me was gone, stolen from my backpack. "We always get our man," is RCMP's famous saying. This time they failed. So much for proclamations!

There are several manufacturers of the single action type revolver. The most sensible handgun for those who are not familiar with the workings of a firearm is a double-action revolver. No slide to pull back, no magazine to lose, or on-off safety. It all matters when the adrenaline is high. All one needs to do with a double-action revolver is aim and pull the trigger. For an expert shot, caliber.22 is sufficient. For those who are not, a .38 Special or larger will help compensate. Sturm/Ruger makes a compact.357 Magnum hand gun that will also accommodate the .38 Special cartridges. Smith & Wesson, Charter Arms, Colt, and a number of other companies offer compact lightweight revolvers. The most complicated and unsafe handgun for the inexperienced is a hammerless automatic, a pistol without a visible hammer. The most dangerous moment while handling a firearm is when the gun is being loaded and unloaded. Always turn away from others during these procedures.

It would take an Act of Congress to invalidate all the laws written on carrying a handgun in each state. As far as the law is concerned, carrying a handgun in the states I crossed seemed permissible, though I was never really sure on horseback. It is virtually impossible to read and remember all the laws regarding guns in every state. Common sense will play a role in retaining your freedom on horseback.

Firearms should be visible and unloaded when entering a township. When I travel horseback through a state other than Oklahoma, where I reside, I fall back on the Second Amendment to the Constitution. For example, if I am in Montana, chances are the Oklahoma law on carrying a handgun will not coincide with the handgun law of Montana. If being an Oklahoman is not sufficient, then being an American should be. When dealing with guns and rights, logic is not always the judgment of a court.

How the Self-Defense Act, the right to carry a concealed weapon, will affect the future is unknown. But, even if one feels slighted by having to pay for what the Second Amendment already allows, the act is still a good thing. After all, self-preservation is, and will always be, a requirement of a higher law.

Prepare for coming in contact with people who will not share your point of view. If you are traveling long distance on horseback, it should be obvious by the way you are dressed, backpack, saddlebags and roll, that you are simply passing through. Do not enter a house or store wearing a gun. It is not something you can take for granted in this day and time.

Logbook: October 8, 1984 Raton, New Mexico
A hard trek down the foothills of Raton Pass. I'm in a McDonald's. Just finished a Big Breakfast and was so starved I ordered another one. With people watching, I tied my horse, came in and sat at this booth. Suddenly, all the people were gone. Must be the gun, I thought, so I took it off. Within a silent minute the Manager appeared, sticking his head around the corner. He asked me if I had a gun. I told him yes and showed him the rig beside me. Then, feeling more explanation was needed, I pointed at my horse Najah through the window and told him, "I'm on horseback... on my way to Mexico."

He shook my hand and told me of news headlines I had not read. A shooting had taken place at a McDonald's somewhere back east and people had been killed. Then, it dawned on me why all the people had scattered. They had seen my gun and had read the same story. I handed the rolled up gun and knife to the Manager. With a relieved smile he put it away for safekeeping. "No biggy," he said. "They'll all come back."

An unloaded gun is a useless mechanical device.

It will be helpful for anyone taking a long ride to have a way of entertaining themselves and maybe others along the way. You need some way to open a conversation. I play the harmonica and do gun tricks. A person with the ability for breaking the ice with strangers might wind up at the supper table. I never knew if my horse liked it or not, but he was pretty much a captive audience whenever I decided to play. I do remember his ears twitching a lot when I pulled out my harmonica and blew a note. And then, for some reason, when I began to play his ears would sag.

When I was a kid, I knew an old guy who made a few coins by playing spoons on his knees. I think his dreams were all in a bottle. Hey! There may come a time when a saddle bum will have to go to work. But don't let it get you. I fixed flats in California, pitched hay in Colorado and tuned up a car in West Virginia.

Jerry L. Bean of Union Missouri, wrote, printed and published *The Union Tribune;* he delivered it as well. Jerry bought me a hamburger and ice cream, and I helped him deliver papers while he interviewed me for a story. A little PR can be helpful.

There are few areas in America today as primitive as the interior of Glacier National Park, through which I made my way south into Lewis and Clark National Forest and beyond. I cut a few fences and shish kabobed a couple of rattlesnakes. A third rattler was short and fat and stuffed with gophers. I passed on that one and from then on stuck with roasted rabbits and crow until I reached White River National Forest. Because of bad weather, it took a week to get through the 1,941,076 acres of wilderness.

It is natural to romanticize while reading or looking at a photograph of someone else who has lived an adventure on horseback. What that instant in time cannot reveal is before and after when there was no food or water, no shower for days, plenty of bugs and mosquitoes and unpredictable weather.

My horse Najah and I were caught in a bad hailstorm. We were in Montana, wide-open country and there was no shelter, not a tree or bush, nothing. All we could do was stand and take it. I kept a tight rein and stayed mounted. I pulled my collar up and leaned forward to block the golf-ball size hail from hitting Najah's head. To keep him from bolting in fear, I talked to him and stroked him hard. When it was over, hail was thick over the ground. I looked back and realized that we had been pounded off our path, one painful step at a time, for nearly fifty yards.

A pack animal can be heaven or hell-sent. If you have a mule and a horse that get along well as a team, and if you don't mind traveling super slow, then take a pack animal. You can ride them alternately. But then, there is another body to watch after and feed.

John Egenes & Spivey near Kelso, California 1973. The following year Egenes started a new ride without a pack animal and ended at Virginia Beach, Virginia.

 js

229

Spivey & Najah – In Montana and headed for Old Mexico, 1984   *js*

What I carried

One afternoon, while rummaging through boxes of junk in the rear of a surplus store, I came upon a box containing thirty World War II canvas flare pouches. The small, stiff-bottom containers had brass zippers and leather tabs and looked like miniature shaving kits. I purchased the whole box and after cutting out the inside flare loops, that's exactly what one of them became. Three others were just right for ammunition, first-aid, and miscellaneous items.

It never occurred to me to write down what I took on my first ride. I started out with more than I should have and realized at the end, what I had at that moment, was all that was needed. Before the Canada-to-Mexico ride I made a list of what I carried.

On horseback, each item carried takes on the same importance as, *one of a kind.*

- *Supply's for traveling on horseback* -

EMERGENCY FOOD: Salt and pepper mixed together and referred to as *gunpowder* in flip-top container. (Screw-on lids are easily lost.) Dehydrated trail meat (beef and pork) Granola bars (various flavors) trail mix (nuts and mixed fruits) a fork and spoon.

POUCH 1: Concentrated facial cleansing liquid (8-oz. container, for washing hair, hands, face and shaving) toothbrush (shortened handle) toothpaste razor, scissors (stainless slide-open mini-snips) tweezers and dental floss.

POUCH 2: Rubbing alcohol (2 oz. container with lift-up spout) water purifying tablets (two small bottles) aspirin, adhesive tape, bandages, lip balm, A & D ointment, snakebite kit, mink oil and vitamins.

POUCH 3 & 4: Matches (book and stick) hairbrush (small) binoculars (8x21 small folding type with neck string and case) fish hooks (several small three-way hooks and nylon line) safety pins (two or more) screwdrivers (key size for guns, standard for hoof pick) camera (35mm with strap and carrying case) Film (5 rolls Ektachrome color slides, 64 ASA) cup (stainless steel, wire handle) can opener (GI type) pliers (long-nose) flashlight (1.5 volts C battery) compass & maps (first leg of ride, on scale of 1:250,000) harmonica (with neck string) logbook (with zipper covers) one ballpoint pen and a book of postage stamps.

SADDLE POUCH, TACK & ATTIRE: Jacket (Levi with customized, fur collar) cap (knit) coat (down-filled, with hood) gloves (leather) trousers (two pair Levi) socks (five pair cushion-sole white cotton) shorts (four pair white cotton) hand towel (white cotton) tissue paper (folded) daypack (two zipper shelves and cushioned shoulder straps) T-shirts (four polo) spurs (bronze, medium rowels) shirts (two long-sleeved cotton) boots (round toe, sixteen-inch tops) waist belt (leather, with holes full length of belt) leash (nylon ribbon, twenty five feet) hat (customized chin-strap and hat band) bandanna (large cotton) sleeping bag (Down, mummy with stuff bag) poncho (light weight with snap-together seams and hood) canteen (flat round, leather covered with shoulder strap, sixty fl. oz.)

ARMS & AMMO: A .45 Colt single action Army 5 1/2-inch barrel, belt with cartridge loops and holster. 50 rounds, .45 long Colt. 20 rounds, .410 cut-down shotgun shells. A Browning 92, lever action carbine. 40 rounds, .44 Remington magnum. A .22 five-shot derringer. 50 rounds, .22 long rifle. A two-blade pocketknife with leather punch. A Sabertooth sheath knife with saw-tooth spine.

SADDLE: Customized, tie-down straps, wool lined, sweat pads, saddlebags, rifle-boot, and covered stirrups. Hair pad, saddle blanket, reins, bridle and bit. A leather whip braided with wrist-loop.

I started the first ride in 1968 with one hundred dollars. It lasted until I reached Manitou Springs, over the Colorado Rockies. I sold the packsaddle I had mailed ahead, along with a Browning automatic pistol, which gave me enough money to continue the ride. When I reached Washington, D. C., I had forty-three cents in my pocket. But born lucky, *National Geographic Society* paid me up front for half the price of a story that I later wrote.

For the ride in 1984, I started out with three hundred and fifty dollars cash. Before that was gone, I found two hundred dollars on a recently mowed shoulder of road in New Mexico, and got a check for one hundred and fifty dollars from home. When I reached Mexico, I still had fifty bucks.

A rider should feel comfortable with four to five hundred dollars tucked away throughout his gear.

Boots are a prime consideration for the trail rider. On an extended journey, pointed-toe boots are far too confining and can play the devil with a rider's feet. Boots of tough slick leather are far superior to those of rough-out leather. The latter becomes too soft and absorbs water instantly.

My cowhide chaps came in handy a couple of times on the '68 ride, but were not worth their weight on the '84 trek. On a long ride chaps are seldom needed and are especially heavy, when wet.

Spurs saved my horse and me more than once. No amount of talking, shouting, or leg pressure can guide and move a horse as effectively as a properly used set of spurs. I found it more to my comfort and safety to do away with the spur heel chain. The heel chain holds the spur snug to the boot and while leading a horse over rugged terrain secured spurs can be dangerous. In a ravine or on the soft grade of a hill, a spur may be caught beneath a root or against a rocky ledge. The trek could end there with a broken ankle and a bad trampling by a frightened horse. It is best to let spurs rise and fall freely while traveling on horseback. On controlled or routine excursions, like on the farm, rent-a-horse, Grand Canyon trail tour, etc., spurs are seldom needed

I did not take a brush. I massaged Najah's back with my bare hands. There is no way a rider can carry everything that would be useful on a cross-country ride, but whenever possible, take items that are multi functional. For example, lip balm can be used for cuts, sunburn, leather conditioner, stitching string wax, gun grease, water repellent for seams of boot soles, bit-burn on your horse's mouth. A hatband can, become a string for hanging up a wet sleeping bag, replacement leather for a saddle strap, a canteen holder, or a tourniquet. In a pinch, one can write with the lead-head of a bullet.

During the 1968 ride, I fashioned an open skillet to cook elk steaks from a strand of barbed wire. The wire was shaped somewhat like an inverted V with a mashed handle of rolled wire. Two short strands were used for closing down on the raw steaks so that it could be rotated without losing the meat. It was all made easier with a pair of long-nose pliers that I carried for cutting wire.

I did mean to carry a hoof pick, but when the '84 ride began, the hoof pick was nowhere to be found. But the third day out into Montana, I found an old screwdriver that I used throughout the journey.

I started out carrying about three gallons of grain. In three days it was gone. Najah could only graze and from then on, it was all by chance. I usually had to buy fifty pounds of feed when we reached a three-day camp site. Sometimes we left grain behind.

Cut-down .410 shells & .45 long Colt cartridges. Spurs with no heel chains. 📷 *js*

What's New

The problem with writing about *what's new* is, by the time the information is published, it has become *what's old*. Even so, the following may yet be relevant.

Since my first ride, everything has changed. Many new products have come into being that can make a cross-country ride easier. The signs of the times always show up in the ditches along the roads.

In 1968, it was eight-track cartridges trashed in the bar ditch. On the second ride, it was cassette tapes dangling in the weeds. Now it is mini-cassettes, floppy discs and CD's strewn from ocean to ocean. I'll be glad when it's only microchips. They'll blend in a lot better with the surroundings.

On the ride from Oklahoma City to Santa Fe, and in Africa, I carried a mini-cassette recorder. I was a little apprehensive about having to depend on batteries, but after considering the small flashlight I had carried on my first ride, I decided to give it a try. It worked out better than I thought it would. I was able to ride and record at the same time. Carrying a logbook requires one to write, and writing can only be done while camped and then, when one is tired, it is tough to recall and write down all the events of the day.

My recordings are still as clear as the day they were made. On them, I can hear the wind, running water, jackals yelping, and the screeching of a distant hawk. So, if you trust a battery, take a recorder and use a note pad for backup.

During the planning of my first ride, when I learned that I had secured the loan of a horse, I began calling others who might assist. Eastman Kodak furnished me with an Instamatic S-20, several rolls of 126 Color slides and a Super-8 movie camera. I seldom got to use Super-8 for having to ship it ahead. Kelty Pack and Levi Strauss were obvious candidates and they too helped supply the project.

When I lost my mule, I shipped my movie camera ahead. I missed some incredible images. It was only at major mail stops that I used the Super-8. Today, video cameras are so compact and lightweight, and the event of a long ride so rare, a horseman should seriously consider taking one.

If one wants to carry a revolver and a rifle, it is common to find them in matching caliber.

If one is concerned about getting lost, tiny beepers can be worn and can be picked up and pinpointed by satellite. Similar methods are used for communication and are commonplace for tracking grizzlies. If anyone feels that they have enough courage to let a bear get close enough, pepper spray is something to consider.

One can now get computerized hand-held devices that let a person know where they are at any given time, as well as show the right direction to go. It can also be used for preseason scouting or mapping a favorite campsite.

There are items like the pocket-sized multi-purpose tool. This handy little device eliminates the need for carrying individual implements such as wire-cutters, pocketknife, leather punch, pliers, etc. Several companies manufacture a multi-purpose tool; some are imports. The one I have was made in the U. S.

Sunglasses were always a big bother to me. I could never keep them for long. They are better now; the degree of ultra-violet protection is greater than it used to be. They come in a various styles, some suitable for the equestrian.

Sunscreens are very popular. They can protect your skin from irreparable damage. Personally, I would not ride one day plastered with any of it. A quality hat with a three and a half-inch wide brim, a bandanna and gloves is what I prefer.

In the event a rider is starting out from scratch and plans one day to really rough it, he or she should familiarize themselves with ways of living off the land. *The Book of Woodcraft, Complete Book of Outdoor Lore* and the standard *Boy Scout Manual* are the ones I'm familiar with. On my first ride, I carried a pamphlet called *Edible & Useful Plants of the West*. I did consult the priceless little book on several occasions, but I'm not sure what happened to it. I may have lost or eaten it somewhere along the

way. A two-week vacationer need not worry about edible plants. Now days, if one does not mind taking some of the adventure out of their adventure, drop a cell phone in your saddlebag.

Due to limiting factors of the long ride, I did not record all the names of the good people who befriended me along the way. However, each person was an equal part of the circumstances that made the journey possible and I thank them all for being there.

I'll saddle up and I'll be free, I'll find a dreamer just like me.
We'll ride where we have never been, and we'll be drinkers of the wind.

The End

Come Little Children

Come little children and ride with me.
Come little children and see what I see.
All that I'll show you will never again be,
the golden green valleys, blue water running free.

Our fathers were builders, hard times they did know.
They built the mighty cities, because they loved us so.
But a new time is coming, it says so in the wind,
and you are the promise of the new life we win.

Come little children and listen to me.
Your future great challenge is one to be free.
Things are never as we wish them to be,
but no life's worth living if you can't live it free.

Here the wind blowing, the calling of the crow.
Listen to a crying child, then you will know.
That everything you're hearing is part of nature's song
and though it's ever changing, with it you belong.

Come little children, there's so much to know.
It's just the beginning, we've so far to go.
Your destiny is the universe that's part of nature's plan
and the brightest star of the journey is no more than a grain of sand.
So, come little children, ride with me.
Come little children and see what I see.

Ocean to Ocean Horseshoes

Mr. Sol wore out eight sets of shoes. *Set 1 & 2,* are unaccounted for.
Set 1, From Santa Barbara, California to Peach Springs, Arizona.
Set 2, From Peach Springs to Tuba City, Arizona.
The following six sets were given as gifts during and after the 1968 ride.
Set 3: From (near) Tuba City, Arizona to Alamosa, Colorado.
Ted Jewell, 1224 North Orange Drive, Hollywood, California.
Set 4: From Alamosa, Colorado to Scott City, Kansas.
Ralph Goodall, IAHA, 224 East Olive, Burbank, California.
Set 5: From Scott City, Kansas to Jefferson City, Missouri.
Bill Boyer, Publisher, Grove-Gazette, Grove City, Kansas.
Set 6: From Jefferson City, Missouri to Portsmouth, Ohio.
Ray Rich, Publisher, Horse & Rider Magazine, Covina, California.
Set 7: From Portsmouth, Ohio to Fort Myer, Virginia.
George & Edith Rosenberg, Abbeville, South Carolina.
Set 8: From Fort Myer, Virginia to Rehoboth Beach, Delaware.
Jefferson Spivey, 6006 Lexington Avenue, Hollywood, California.

Set 8: Worn by Mr. Sol, ended the 1968 ride. Sixteen years later, in
1984, the same shoes worn by Najah began the Canada to Mexico ride.
Rose Araby Mr. Sol AHCR # 29338
Foaled May 22, 1964
Sire: Silver Crescent 6273
Dam: Jawharah 2857
Rose Araby Arabians, Abbeville, South Carolina.

FROM THE DESK OF
LUCKY SIMPSON

June 17, 1968

Jeff Spivey

Dear Sir:

    With much personal interest I was glad to become
acquainted with you and your Rose Grey Arabian gelding,
"Mr. Sol". In talking with you and examining Mr. Sol,
I feel that both of you have undertaken a very extensive
project the results of which are yet to be seen.

    Mr. Sol is showing some signs of fatigue as you
have neared the halfway mark of your cross-the-nation
ride. This is to be expected as you have the worst
deserts and the highest mountains behind you. The fact
that your Arabian has made this much of the trip without
the benefit of grain in the ration is evidence of the
endurance for which Arabians are famous.

    Your plans to stop here for more than a week are
to the advantage of both of you. Mr. Sol needs to
build up some for the last half of the trip.

    The only precautions I would make are to watch the
hoofs which at this stage are not in trouble, but which
show some injury and to attempt to use a high calorie
diet - preferably with grain. Knowing your overall
plans I would assume that you will make the rest of the
trip without grain but punctuated by the proper rest
stops - such as this one here.

    With the best of luck to the both of you on the
remainder of the journey, I remain

Sincerely,

Dr. Lucky Simpson, D.V.M.
Fountain, Colorado

LS /mrs

Index

Jefferson Spivey